ARTIFICIAL INTELLIGENCE AND ITS TRANSFORMATIVE IMPACT ON HEALTHCARE

Aakash Jain
Akanksha Pathak

PREFACE

Artificial intelligence (AI) has revolutionized numerous industries, and healthcare is no exception. The transformative impact of AI on healthcare has been witnessed in various aspects, including medical imaging, drug discovery and development, clinical decision-making, patient monitoring and management, and many others. With its potential to improve the efficiency and accuracy of healthcare services, AI is seen as a promising solution to many challenges faced by the healthcare industry, including the rising cost of healthcare and the increasing demand for personalized and patient-centered care.

This book provides a comprehensive overview of the applications of AI in healthcare, from understanding the evolution of AI in healthcare to exploring its limitations and future possibilities. It covers a range of topics, including the advantages and disadvantages of AI, the various applications of AI in healthcare, patient care, revenue cycle management, security and privacy, challenges and limitations, and the future of AI in healthcare. Additionally, case studies and practical applications of AI in healthcare are presented to illustrate the real-world impact of this technology on the healthcare industry.

This book is aimed at healthcare professionals, researchers, policymakers, and anyone interested in understanding how AI is transforming the healthcare industry. It provides valuable insights into the potential benefits of AI in healthcare, as well as the challenges and limitations that must be addressed to fully realize its potential. With its comprehensive coverage of the topic, this book is an essential resource for anyone interested in the future of healthcare.

CONTENTS

CHAPTER 1:
UNDERSTANDING AI
IN HEALTHCARE

C hapter 1 of the book introduces AI in healthcare. It aims to define AI and its various applications in healthcare. It also explores the potential of AI to transform healthcare. Artificial Intelligence (AI) has become one of the most transformative technologies in the healthcare industry, and it has been revolutionizing the way healthcare providers deliver patient care. AI has the potential to improve healthcare outcomes, lower costs, and increase efficiency.

The Evolution Of Artificial Intelligence In Healthcare

Artificial Intelligence (AI) has been transforming the healthcare industry for several decades. The evolution of AI in healthcare has been marked by significant advances in technology, research, and implementation. From early rule-based systems to sophisticated deep learning algorithms, AI has become a critical tool in improving healthcare outcomes for patients. This chapter will explore the history of AI in healthcare and the key milestones that have led to its current state.

Early Developments in Artificial Intelligence & Healthcare

The first developments in AI for healthcare can be traced back to the 1950s, when computer scientists began exploring the potential of machine learning and decision-making algorithms. These early AI systems were rule-based, relying on predetermined algorithms and decision trees to analyze data and make recommendations. One of the earliest examples of AI in healthcare was the MYCIN system, which was developed in the 1970s to assist in the diagnosis of bacterial infections. MYCIN was a rule-based system that used a set of algorithms to analyze patient symptoms and provide treatment recommendations. While MYCIN was considered a groundbreaking development at the time, it had several limitations, including a lack of flexibility and an inability to adapt to new data.

In the 1980s and 1990s, researchers began exploring the potential of neural networks for healthcare applications. Neural networks are a type of machine learning that uses interconnected nodes to analyze data and identify patterns. One early example of neural networks in healthcare was the development of the Quick Medical Reference (QMR) system in the late 1980s. QMR was a neural network-based system that used patient data to predict the likelihood of various medical conditions. While QMR showed promise, it was limited by the availability and quality of data, which was often incomplete or inaccurate.

Advances in Artificial Intelligence and Healthcare

In the 2000s, the availability of large datasets and advances in computing power led to significant advances in AI for healthcare. One of the most significant developments was the introduction of support vector machines (SVMs), which are a type of machine learning algorithm that can be used for classification and regression analysis. SVMs were used in a wide range of healthcare applications, including the diagnosis of breast cancer, the detection of Alzheimer's disease, and the prediction of patient outcomes.

Another significant development in AI for healthcare was the introduction of deep learning, which is a type of machine learning that uses artificial neural networks to analyze large datasets. Deep learning algorithms are able to identify complex patterns in data and make predictions with a high degree of accuracy. Deep learning has been used in a wide range of healthcare applications, including medical imaging, drug discovery, and personalized medicine.

One of the most promising applications of AI in healthcare is medical imaging. Medical imaging is a critical tool in the diagnosis and treatment of many medical conditions, but it is often limited by the ability of radiologists to interpret complex images. AI has the potential to improve the accuracy and efficiency of medical imaging by automating image analysis and providing more accurate diagnoses.

In recent years, there have been significant advances in AI for medical imaging. One of the most promising applications is in the analysis of medical images for the detection of diseases such as cancer. Deep learning algorithms have been used to analyze large datasets of medical images, including X-rays, CT scans, and MRIs. These algorithms are able to identify subtle patterns and features in the images that may be missed by human radiologists.

Another promising application of AI in medical imaging is in the analysis of medical data for personalized medicine. AI algorithms can analyze large datasets of medical records and genetic data to identify the most effective treatments for individual patients based on their unique medical history, genetics, and lifestyle factors.

Another area where AI has the potential to revolutionize healthcare is in drug discovery. Developing new drugs is a complex and expensive process that often takes years and involves extensive testing and research. AI has the potential to streamline the drug discovery process by identifying potential drug candidates more quickly and accurately than traditional methods.

One application of AI in drug discovery is in the identification of new targets for drug development. AI algorithms can analyze large datasets of biological information to identify new drug targets based on molecular interactions, gene expression patterns, and other factors. These algorithms can also be used to identify potential side effects and interactions with other drugs, helping to reduce the risk of adverse reactions.

Another application of AI in drug discovery is in the prediction of drug efficacy and toxicity. AI algorithms can analyze large datasets of drug data to identify the most effective treatments for specific diseases and patient populations. These algorithms can also predict potential side effects and toxicity, helping to identify potential safety issues before drugs are tested on human subjects.

Challenges and Limitations of AI in Healthcare

While AI has the potential to revolutionize healthcare, there are also significant challenges and limitations that must be addressed. One of the biggest challenges is the lack of standardized data and interoperability between healthcare systems. Many healthcare systems use different data formats and have limited interoperability, making it difficult to share data between systems and analyze large datasets.

Another challenge is the need for ethical and responsible use of AI in healthcare. AI algorithms can be biased or make inaccurate predictions if they are trained on incomplete or biased datasets. It is important for healthcare providers and researchers to carefully consider the potential risks and drawbacks of AI and to develop strategies to address any potential issues.

Finally, there is a need for ongoing research and development to improve the accuracy and efficiency of AI in healthcare. While AI has shown promise in a wide range of applications, there is still much to learn about how to effectively integrate AI into healthcare systems and ensure that it is used responsibly and ethically.

Developments of AI in healthcare has been rapid and exciting, with a wide range of applications and potential benefits. From improving diagnostic accuracy to streamlining administrative tasks, AI has the potential to transform healthcare delivery and improve patient outcomes.

As the use of AI in healthcare continues to grow, it is important for healthcare providers and researchers to address the challenges and limitations of AI and to ensure that it is used responsibly and ethically. This will require ongoing research and development, as well as collaboration between healthcare providers, researchers, and technology companies.

Ultimately, the goal of AI in healthcare should be to improve patient outcomes and to enhance the quality and efficiency of healthcare delivery. With careful planning and responsible use, AI has the potential to achieve these goals and to transform healthcare delivery for the better.

Types Of Artificial Intelligence In Healthcare

Artificial intelligence (AI) is a rapidly evolving technology that has the potential to transform healthcare delivery. From improving diagnostic accuracy to streamlining administrative tasks, AI has a wide range of applications in healthcare. In this chapter, we will explore the different types of AI in healthcare and their potential benefits.

Rule-based Systems

Rule-based systems are a type of artificial intelligence (AI) systems that operate on a set of predefined rules and decision-making algorithms to analyze data and generate recommendations or make decisions. These systems are built based on expert knowledge and domain-specific rules that are designed to mimic human decision-making processes. By encoding these rules into the system, it can effectively process large amounts of data and provide accurate assessments and recommendations in a consistent manner.

In the field of healthcare, rule-based systems can be utilized to analyze electrocardiogram (ECG) data for diagnosing heart disease. The system would be programmed with a set of rules derived from medical guidelines and expert knowledge in cardiology. These rules would define the patterns and abnormalities in ECG signals that are indicative of various heart conditions. When presented with a new ECG data, the system would evaluate the data against the rules and generate a diagnosis or a recommendation based on the findings.

One of the advantages of rule-based systems is their transparency and interpretability. Since the rules are explicitly defined, it is possible to trace the decision-making process and understand why a particular recommendation or decision was made. This transparency is particularly important in critical domains like healthcare, where the reasoning behind the system's output is crucial for gaining trust and acceptance from medical professionals. Furthermore, rule-based systems can be updated easily by modifying or adding new rules, allowing them to adapt to evolving knowledge and guidelines in the respective field.

However, rule-based systems also have limitations. They heavily rely on the accuracy and completeness of the predefined rules, which means that any gaps or inaccuracies in the rules can lead to incorrect recommendations. Developing and maintaining these rules can be a complex and time-consuming task, requiring expert knowledge and domain expertise. Additionally, rule-based systems may struggle to handle uncertainty or ambiguity, as they operate based on rigid rules and may not have the ability to weigh different pieces of evidence or consider contextual information. Therefore, while rule-based systems can be effective in certain applications, they may not be suitable for domains that involve complex or uncertain scenarios.

Robotic Process Automation

Robotic Process Automation (RPA) is another AI technology that automates repetitive, rule-based tasks by mimicking human interactions with computer systems and applications. RPA systems are designed to perform tasks that are highly structured, rule-driven, and require little to no cognitive decision-making. These systems operate by following predefined rules and instructions, often in the form of workflows, to interact with user interfaces, extract and manipulate data, and perform actions across different software systems.

In the healthcare industry, RPA can be applied to streamline administrative tasks and enhance operational efficiency. For instance, RPA can be utilized to automate the process of verifying patient insurance eligibility. This typically involves checking patient information against insurance databases, confirming coverage, and ensuring compliance with specific rules and requirements. RPA can be programmed to extract patient data from electronic health records (EHRs), interact with insurance portals, and perform the necessary verification steps. By automating this process, healthcare providers can save time and reduce errors, allowing staff to focus on patient care instead of administrative tasks.

One of the key advantages of RPA is its ability to work with existing IT infrastructure without requiring extensive changes or integrations. RPA systems can interact with applications and systems through the same user interfaces that humans use, making them flexible and easily deployable. Additionally, RPA can work 24/7 without interruptions, leading to improved efficiency and productivity. Since RPA operates based on predefined rules and workflows, it also ensures consistency and accuracy in task execution.

However, RPA also has limitations. It is not suitable for tasks that involve complex decision-making, unstructured data, or require high-level cognitive abilities. RPA is designed for rule-based, repetitive tasks and lacks the ability to handle ambiguity, adapt to changing situations, or make judgment calls. Furthermore, RPA systems require well-defined and stable processes to work effectively. Any changes in the underlying systems or interfaces may require updates to the RPA workflows, which can introduce additional maintenance overhead.

Machine Learning

Machine learning is a type of AI that involves training algorithms on large datasets to identify patterns and make predictions. In healthcare, machine learning algorithms can be used for a wide range of applications, including diagnostic imaging, drug discovery, and personalized treatment recommendations.

One example of machine learning in healthcare is the use of computer-aided diagnosis (CAD) systems for interpreting medical images, such as X-rays and MRIs. CAD systems use machine learning algorithms to analyze images and identify potential abnormalities, helping to improve diagnostic accuracy and reduce the risk of false negatives.

Machine learning algorithms can also be used in drug discovery to identify potential drug candidates and predict their efficacy and safety. By analyzing large datasets of biological and chemical information, machine learning algorithms can identify potential drug targets and predict the likelihood of success for specific drug candidates.

Natural Language Processing

Natural language processing (NLP) is a type of AI that involves analyzing and interpreting human language. In healthcare, NLP can be used to analyze electronic health records (EHRs), patient notes, and other text-based data to identify potential trends and patterns.

One application of NLP in healthcare is the analysis of clinical notes to identify potential adverse events or side effects associated with specific treatments. By analyzing large datasets of clinical notes, NLP algorithms can identify potential safety issues and help healthcare providers make more informed treatment decisions.

NLP can also be used to improve the accuracy of coding and billing for healthcare services. By analyzing EHR data, NLP algorithms can identify potential errors or discrepancies in coding and billing, helping to reduce the risk of fraud and ensure that healthcare providers are properly reimbursed for their services.

Robotics

Robotic systems are another type of AI that has the potential to transform healthcare delivery. In healthcare, robots can be used for a wide range of applications, including surgical procedures, rehabilitation, and patient monitoring.

One example of robotics in healthcare is the use of surgical robots for minimally invasive procedures. Surgical robots use advanced sensors and imaging systems to provide surgeons with real-time feedback during procedures, helping to improve surgical precision and reduce the risk of complications.

Robotic systems can also be used for patient monitoring and rehabilitation. For example, robotic exoskeletons can be used to help patients with mobility issues regain strength and mobility, while robotic systems can be used for remote monitoring of patients with chronic conditions.

Expert Systems

Expert systems are AI systems that are designed to replicate the decision-making capabilities of human experts. In healthcare, expert systems can be used for diagnostic decision-making, treatment planning, and other clinical applications.

One example of an expert system in healthcare is the use of clinical decision support systems (CDSS) to provide healthcare providers with real-time recommendations and alerts based on patient data. CDSS systems can analyze patient data to identify potential risks or complications and provide healthcare providers with evidence-based recommendations for treatment.

Expert systems can also be used to improve the accuracy of diagnostic decision-making. For example, expert systems can be used to analyze medical images and provide healthcare providers with real-time feedback and recommendations based on the characteristics of the images.

Generative Artificial Intelligence

Generative AI refers to AI systems that have the ability to generate new content, such as images, text, or even entire scenarios, based on patterns and examples from existing data. In the context of healthcare, generative AI can be applied to various tasks, including medical image synthesis, drug discovery, and clinical data generation.

One example of generative AI in healthcare is the synthesis of medical images. Generative models, such as generative adversarial networks (GANs), can be trained on a large dataset of medical images to learn the underlying patterns and generate new, realistic images. This can be particularly useful in situations where there is a shortage of labeled data or when there is a need to augment existing datasets. By generating synthetic medical images, it is possible to create larger and more diverse datasets for training and testing algorithms, which can ultimately improve the accuracy and performance of image-based diagnostics and treatments.

Another application of generative AI in healthcare is in drug discovery. Discovering new drugs is a complex and time-consuming process. Generative models can be employed to generate novel chemical structures that have the potential to exhibit desired properties, such as efficacy against specific diseases or improved safety profiles. By training the models on existing chemical databases and utilizing reinforcement learning or other optimization techniques, generative AI can propose new molecules that can be further evaluated and potentially developed into new therapeutic agents. This approach has the potential to accelerate the drug discovery process and provide novel treatment options for various medical conditions.

Generative AI can also be used to generate synthetic clinical data for research and analysis purposes. By training the models on large datasets of patient records, generative AI algorithms can generate synthetic patient profiles that preserve the statistical characteristics and patterns of real-world data. This synthesized data can then be used for various applications, such as evaluating the effectiveness of treatment strategies, conducting simulations, or testing algorithms and models without violating patient privacy or data protection regulations.

While generative AI holds significant promise in healthcare, it is crucial to ensure the ethical and responsible use of such technologies. Generating synthetic medical data or images must be done with caution, considering the potential risks associated with biases, privacy concerns, and the potential impact on patient outcomes. Thorough validation and evaluation of the generated content are essential to ensure the reliability and safety of the applications built on generative AI in healthcare.

What's Next?

The different types of AI in healthcare all have the potential to transform healthcare delivery and improve patient outcomes. From machine learning algorithms for drug discovery to robotic systems for patient monitoring and rehabilitation, AI has the potential to revolutionize healthcare delivery in a wide range of applications.

As the use of AI in healthcare continues to grow, it is important for healthcare providers and researchers to work together to ensure that AI is used ethically and responsibly. This includes ensuring that AI systems are transparent, reliable, and unbiased, and that patient data is protected and used in accordance with ethical and legal standards.

Furthermore, it is important to recognize that AI is not a replacement for human expertise and judgment. Rather, AI should be seen as a tool to support and augment human decision-making, helping healthcare providers to make more informed and accurate diagnoses, treatment plans, and other clinical decisions.

As the field of AI in healthcare continues to evolve, it is likely that we will see new types of AI emerge and new applications of existing AI technologies. However, by understanding the different types of AI in healthcare and their potential benefits and limitations, we can work towards a future where AI is used to improve healthcare delivery and enhance patient outcomes.

Advantages Of Artificial Intelligence In Healthcare

As with any emerging technology, the use of AI in healthcare comes with both advantages and disadvantages. In this section, we will delve into the numerous advantages associated with the integration of AI in healthcare. Let's explore some of the key benefits offered by this emerging technology.

Improved Diagnosis and Treatment

One of the main advantages of AI in healthcare is its potential to improve diagnosis and treatment. AI algorithms can analyze vast amounts of patient data, including medical records, imaging scans, and genetic information, to identify patterns and make predictions about a patient's health status. This can help healthcare providers to make more accurate diagnoses and develop more effective treatment plans.

For example, AI algorithms can be used to analyze medical images and identify abnormalities that may be missed by human radiologists. This can lead to earlier detection and treatment of diseases, such as cancer.

Increased Efficiency

Another advantage of AI in healthcare is its potential to increase efficiency. AI algorithms can automate many routine tasks, such as data entry and analysis, freeing up healthcare providers to focus on more complex tasks that require human expertise and judgment.

For example, AI chatbots can be used to triage patients and provide basic medical advice, reducing the workload of healthcare providers and enabling them to focus on more urgent cases.

Personalized Medicine

AI in healthcare also has the potential to support personalized medicine. By analyzing a patient's medical history, genetic data, and other relevant information, AI algorithms can develop personalized treatment plans that take into account the patient's individual needs and characteristics.

For example, AI algorithms can be used to identify genetic markers that may indicate a higher risk of certain diseases, such as Alzheimer's disease or heart disease. This information can then be used to develop personalized prevention and treatment strategies.

Cost Savings

Finally, AI in healthcare has the potential to generate significant cost savings. By automating routine tasks and improving efficiency, healthcare providers can reduce their operational costs and improve their bottom line.

For example, AI algorithms can be used to identify patients who are at high risk of hospital readmission, enabling healthcare providers to intervene early and reduce the likelihood of readmission. This can lead to significant cost savings for healthcare providers and insurers.

Disadvantages Of Artificial Intelligence In Healthcare

In this section, we will explore the potential drawbacks and considerations associated with the integration of AI in healthcare. Let's delve into some of the key challenges and disadvantages posed by this emerging technology.

Bias and Discrimination

One of the main concerns with AI in healthcare is the potential for bias and discrimination. AI algorithms are only as unbiased as the data they are trained on, and if the data contains biases or discriminatory patterns, the algorithm will replicate and amplify these biases.

For example, if an AI algorithm is trained on medical data that is biased against certain minority groups, it may be less accurate in diagnosing and treating those groups, leading to disparities in healthcare outcomes.

Lack of Human Interaction

Another potential disadvantage of AI in healthcare is the lack of human interaction. While AI algorithms can automate many routine tasks, they cannot replace the human touch that is essential for building trust and rapport between healthcare providers and patients.

For example, while an AI chatbot may be able to provide basic medical advice, it cannot provide the emotional support and empathy that many patients need when dealing with a health crisis.

Legal and Ethical Concerns

The use of AI in healthcare also raises a number of legal and ethical concerns. For example, who is responsible if an AI algorithm makes a mistake that leads to harm to a patient? What happens if an AI algorithm is used to make life-and-death decisions without adequate human oversight?

Furthermore, the use of AI in healthcare raises concerns about patient privacy and data protection. Healthcare providers must ensure that patient data is collected, stored, and used in accordance with ethical and legal standards, and that patients have control over their own data.

Technical Limitations

AI in healthcare is not without technical limitations. For example, AI algorithms require vast amounts of data to be trained effectively. Collecting and cleaning this data can be a time-consuming process, and it may not always be available. In addition, there are limits to what AI algorithms can learn from the data. They may not be able to identify subtle nuances or contextual factors that a human healthcare provider would pick up on.

Moreover, AI algorithms may not always be transparent, which can be a limitation in the healthcare industry where transparency is important. In some cases, it may be unclear how an AI algorithm arrived at a particular diagnosis or treatment recommendation, making it difficult for healthcare providers to understand and trust the results.

Implementation Challenges

Integrating AI into existing healthcare systems can be a challenging process. AI systems must be designed to work with a wide range of different electronic health record (EHR) systems, which can be complex and differ from one another. Additionally, there may be resistance from healthcare providers who are used to traditional methods of diagnosis and treatment. It can be challenging to train healthcare providers to use AI systems effectively and to gain their trust in the results.

Ethical Concerns

There are also ethical concerns associated with the use of AI in healthcare. For example, AI algorithms may make decisions that are not consistent with a patient's preferences or values. There is also the concern that AI could be used to make decisions that prioritize cost savings over patient care. Finally, there is the question of who is responsible if an AI algorithm makes a mistake that leads to harm or injury.

Risk of Bias

One of the major risks associated with AI in healthcare is the potential for bias. AI algorithms rely on vast amounts of data to train their models, and if that data is biased or incomplete, the resulting algorithm will be too. For example, if an AI algorithm is trained on data that is biased towards certain demographics, it may not be effective at diagnosing or treating patients from other demographics. This can lead to unequal treatment and worsened outcomes for certain groups of patients.

Furthermore, the risk of bias can also extend to the development and deployment of AI in healthcare. For example, the algorithms used may not be transparent, making it difficult to identify and correct biases. Additionally, there may be biases in the selection of data used to train AI algorithms. In some cases, there may be a lack of diversity in the data used, which can lead to biased results.

Addressing the risk of bias is essential for ensuring that AI is used ethically and effectively in healthcare. This can involve ensuring that data used to train AI algorithms is diverse and representative of the patient population. Additionally, AI algorithms should be transparent, allowing healthcare providers to understand how decisions are made. It is also important to have oversight and governance structures in place to ensure that AI is used ethically and in line with patient preferences and values.

Conclusion

AI has the potential to revolutionize healthcare by improving the speed and accuracy of diagnosis, reducing costs, and improving patient outcomes. However, it is essential to recognize the potential limitations and challenges associated with the use of AI in healthcare. It is important to address these challenges to ensure that AI is used effectively and ethically in the healthcare industry. Ultimately, the goal should be to use AI to complement and enhance the expertise of healthcare providers, rather than replace them. By working together, AI and healthcare providers can help to ensure that patients receive the best possible care

CHAPTER 2:
APPLICATIONS OF
AI IN HEALTHCARE

A rtificial intelligence (AI) is transforming healthcare by enabling faster and more accurate diagnosis, improving treatment outcomes, and enhancing patient care. The applications of AI in healthcare are diverse, ranging from medical imaging and diagnosis to precision medicine and personalized care. In this chapter we will explore the different applications of AI in healthcare and the benefits they offer.

Medical Imaging And Diagnosis

Medical imaging is an essential tool for diagnosing and monitoring many different types of medical conditions, from broken bones to cancer. Traditionally, medical imaging has been interpreted by trained human specialists, but in recent years, artificial intelligence (AI) has emerged as a powerful tool for analyzing medical images and assisting with diagnosis.

In this section, we will explore the applications of AI in medical imaging and diagnosis, including the benefits and challenges of using AI for medical image analysis, the different types of AI algorithms used for medical image analysis, and examples of how AI is being used in medical imaging and diagnosis today.

The Benefits and Challenges of Using AI for Medical Image Analysis

The use of AI in medical imaging and diagnosis offers several potential benefits. First, AI can help to improve the accuracy and speed of diagnosis, by analyzing large amounts of medical image data and identifying patterns and anomalies that might be missed by human specialists. This can help to ensure that patients receive timely and accurate diagnoses, improving their chances of successful treatment and recovery.

Second, AI can help to reduce the workload and stress on human specialists, by automating certain tasks such as image analysis and report generation. This can help to improve the efficiency of healthcare delivery, allowing specialists to focus their time and energy on more complex cases and tasks.

However, there are also several challenges associated with the use of AI in medical imaging and diagnosis. One major challenge is ensuring that AI algorithms are accurate and reliable, as errors or biases in AI algorithms can have serious consequences for patient safety. Another challenge is ensuring that AI is used ethically and transparently, with appropriate safeguards in place to protect patient privacy and ensure that healthcare providers are not unfairly influenced by commercial interests.

Types of AI Algorithms Used for Medical Image Analysis

There are several different types of AI algorithms that are used for medical image analysis, each with its own strengths and limitations. Some of the most common types of AI algorithms used for medical image analysis include:

Convolutional Neural Networks (CNNs): CNNs are a type of deep learning algorithm that are particularly well-suited to image analysis tasks. CNNs consist of several layers of interconnected neurons that are trained to identify patterns and features in images, and can be used for tasks such as image segmentation, object detection, and classification.

Recurrent Neural Networks (RNNs): RNNs are another type of deep learning algorithm that are used for sequential data analysis, such as time series or signal data. RNNs can be used for tasks such as image reconstruction and analysis of medical signals, such as electrocardiograms (ECGs).

Support Vector Machines (SVMs): SVMs are a type of machine learning algorithm that are commonly used for classification tasks, such as distinguishing between different types of medical conditions based on imaging data. SVMs work by identifying a boundary or "hyperplane" that separates different classes of data in a high-dimensional space.

Decision Trees: Decision trees are a type of machine learning algorithm that are used for classification and regression tasks. Decision trees work by recursively partitioning the input data into subsets based on the values of different features and can be used to predict the likelihood of different medical conditions based on imaging data.

Examples of AI in Medical Imaging and Diagnosis

There are many examples of how AI is being used in medical imaging and diagnosis today, across a range of different medical conditions and imaging modalities. Some of the most promising applications of AI in medical imaging and diagnosis include:

Detection and Diagnosis of Breast Cancer: Breast cancer is one of the most common forms of cancer among women, and

21

early detection is critical for successful treatment and recovery. AI is being used to analyze mammography images to detect early signs of breast cancer, such as microcalcifications and masses. One example is the use of CNNs to analyze digital mammograms, which has been shown to improve the accuracy of breast cancer detection compared to human specialists alone.

Detection and Diagnosis of Lung Cancer: Lung cancer is another common form of cancer that can be difficult to diagnose early. AI is being used to analyze chest CT scans to detect early signs of lung cancer, such as nodules and masses. One example is the use of CNNs to analyze chest CT scans, which has been shown to improve the accuracy of lung cancer detection compared to human specialists alone.

Detection and Diagnosis of Brain Tumors: Brain tumors are another medical condition that can benefit from the use of AI in medical imaging and diagnosis. AI is being used to analyze MRI scans to detect brain tumors and to classify them based on their type and severity. One example is the use of CNNs to analyze MRI scans of brain tumors, which has been shown to improve the accuracy of diagnosis and classification compared to human specialists alone.

Detection and Diagnosis of Diabetic Retinopathy: Diabetic retinopathy is a complication of diabetes that affects the eyes and can lead to vision loss if left untreated. AI is being used to analyze retinal images to detect early signs of diabetic retinopathy, such as microaneurysms and hemorrhages. One example is the use of CNNs to analyze retinal images, which has been shown to improve the accuracy of diabetic retinopathy detection compared to human specialists alone.

Personalized Treatment Planning: AI is also being used to assist with personalized treatment planning, by analyzing medical images and other patient data to develop customized treatment plans for individual patients. For example, AI can be used to analyze MRI scans to determine the best surgical approach for a patient with a brain tumor, or to analyze CT scans to determine the optimal radiation dose for a patient with lung cancer.

Disease Progression Monitoring: AI can also be used to monitor disease progression over time, by analyzing medical images and other patient data to track changes in disease severity and response to treatment. For example, AI can be used to analyze MRI scans to monitor the progression of multiple sclerosis, or to analyze CT scans to monitor the response of lung cancer to chemotherapy.

Summary: Medical Imaging and Diagnosis

The use of AI in medical imaging and diagnosis offers several potential benefits, including improved accuracy and speed of diagnosis, reduced workload for human specialists, and personalized treatment planning. However, there are also several challenges associated with the use of AI in medical imaging and diagnosis, including ensuring the accuracy and reliability of AI algorithms and ensuring that AI is used ethically and transparently.

Despite these challenges, the potential benefits of AI in medical imaging and diagnosis are too great to ignore. As AI technology continues to evolve and improve, we can expect to see even more exciting applications of AI in medical imaging and diagnosis, transforming the way we diagnose and treat medical conditions and improving patient outcomes.

Drug Discovery And Development

Drug discovery and development is a complex and time-consuming process that involves the identification and testing of potential drug candidates for the treatment of various diseases. Artificial intelligence (AI) has the potential to revolutionize this process, by accelerating drug discovery and development, improving the accuracy of drug design, and reducing the costs associated with drug development.

AI in Drug Discovery and Development

The process of drug discovery and development typically involves several stages, including target identification, lead discovery, lead optimization, preclinical testing, clinical testing, and regulatory approval. AI can be used to improve each of these stages, as described below:

Target Identification: The first stage in drug discovery is identifying potential targets for drug development, such as specific proteins or genes that are involved in the development or progression of a disease. AI can be used to analyze large amounts of biological data, such as genomic data and protein structures, to identify potential targets for drug development. For example, machine learning algorithms can be used to analyze genomic data from cancer patients to identify genetic mutations that are associated with cancer development.

Lead Discovery: Once potential targets have been identified, the next stage is to identify potential drug candidates that can interact with the target and modify its activity. AI can be used to identify potential drug candidates by analyzing large databases of chemical compounds and predicting their potential activity against a specific target. For example, machine learning algorithms can be used to analyze chemical structures and predict their potential binding affinity for a specific protein target.

Lead Optimization: After potential drug candidates have been identified, the next stage is to optimize their chemical structure to improve their activity and reduce any potential side effects.

AI can be used to predict the potential efficacy and toxicity of different chemical structures, and to guide the design of new compounds. For example, machine learning algorithms can be used to predict the potential toxicity of different chemical structures based on their molecular properties.

Preclinical Testing: Once potential drug candidates have been optimized, the next stage is to test their efficacy and toxicity in preclinical models, such as animal models. AI can be used to improve the accuracy and efficiency of preclinical testing by predicting the potential efficacy and toxicity of new drug candidates based on their chemical structures and activity profiles. For example, machine learning algorithms can be used to predict the potential efficacy of new cancer drugs based on their activity against specific genetic mutations.

Clinical Testing: If a drug candidate passes preclinical testing, the next stage is to test its efficacy and safety in human clinical trials. AI can be used to improve the design and analysis of clinical trials, by predicting the potential efficacy and toxicity of new drug candidates and identifying patient populations that are most likely to respond to treatment. For example, machine learning algorithms can be used to predict the potential efficacy of new cancer drugs based on the genetic profile of individual patients.

Regulatory Approval: If a drug candidate is shown to be safe and effective in clinical trials, the final stage is to obtain regulatory approval for its use in the treatment of a specific disease. AI can be used to improve the regulatory approval process by predicting the potential efficacy and safety of new drug candidates, and by identifying potential safety concerns before they arise. For example, machine learning algorithms can be used to predict the potential safety of new drugs based on their molecular properties and activity profiles.

Benefits and Challenges of AI in Drug Discovery and Development

The use of AI in drug discovery and development offers several potential benefits, including:

Faster and more efficient drug discovery and development: AI can help to accelerate the drug discovery and development process by reducing the time and costs associated with each stage of drug development.

More accurate drug design: AI can help to improve the accuracy of drug design by predicting the potential activity and toxicity of new drug candidates based on their chemical structures and activity profiles.

Personalized medicine: AI can help to identify patient populations that are most likely to respond to specific treatments, and to design personalized treatment plans based on individual patient characteristics.

Reduced costs: AI can help to reduce the costs associated with drug development by improving the efficiency of the drug discovery process and by reducing the number of failed clinical trials.

However, there are also several challenges associated with the use of AI in drug discovery and development, including:

Data quality and availability: AI relies on large amounts of high-quality data to make accurate predictions. However, data quality and availability can be a challenge in drug discovery and development, particularly for rare diseases or complex diseases that involve multiple genetic and environmental factors.

Ethical concerns: The use of AI in drug discovery and

development raises ethical concerns, such as the potential for biased algorithms or the use of patient data without informed consent.

Regulatory challenges: The use of AI in drug discovery and development raises regulatory challenges, such as the need to validate AI algorithms and ensure their safety and efficacy.

Integration with existing systems: Integrating AI into existing drug discovery and development processes can be a challenge, particularly in large pharmaceutical companies that have established workflows and systems.

Case Studies of AI in Drug Discovery and Development

Despite these challenges, there have been several successful case studies of AI in drug discovery and development, as described below:

Atomwise: Atomwise is a company that uses AI to predict the potential activity of new drug candidates against specific protein targets. The company uses deep learning algorithms to analyze large databases of chemical compounds and predict their potential binding affinity for a specific protein target. Atomwise has used this approach to identify potential drug candidates for a range of diseases, including Ebola, multiple sclerosis, and cystic fibrosis.

Insilico Medicine: Insilico Medicine is a company that uses AI to design new drugs for a range of diseases, including cancer, aging, and neurological disorders. The company uses deep learning algorithms to analyze large amounts of biological data and predict the potential efficacy and toxicity of new drug candidates. Insilico Medicine has used this approach to design potential drug candidates for a range of diseases, including Alzheimer's disease, nonalcoholic steatohepatitis idiopathic pulmonary fibrosis.

BenevolentAI: BenevolentAI is a company that uses AI to improve the drug discovery and development process by analyzing large amounts of biomedical data, such as clinical trial data and scientific publications. The company uses natural language processing and machine learning algorithms to extract insights from this data and identify potential drug candidates for a range of diseases, including Parkinson's disease, amyotrophic lateral sclerosis, and sarcopenia.

Summary: Drug Discovery and Development

AI has the potential to revolutionize the drug discovery and development process by accelerating drug discovery and development, improving the accuracy of drug design, and reducing the costs associated with drug development. However, there are also several challenges associated with the use of AI in drug discovery and development, including data quality and availability, ethical concerns, regulatory challenges, and integration with existing systems. Despite these challenges, there have been several successful case studies of AI in drug discovery and development, and the use of AI in this field is likely to continue to grow in the coming years.

Clinical Decision Support Systems

Clinical decision support systems (CDSS) are computer-based tools that assist healthcare providers in making clinical decisions. These systems use a variety of technologies, such as artificial intelligence, machine learning, and natural language processing, to analyze patient data and provide recommendations to healthcare providers.

The use of CDSS has the potential to improve patient outcomes, reduce medical errors, and increase the efficiency of healthcare delivery. In this chapter, we will explore the different types of CDSS, their applications in healthcare, and the benefits and challenges associated with their use.

Types of Clinical Decision Support Systems

There are several different types of CDSS, including:

Knowledge-based systems: Knowledge-based systems use a set of rules or algorithms to analyze patient data and provide recommendations to healthcare providers. These systems are based on a predetermined set of rules or guidelines and can be used to support clinical decision-making in a variety of contexts, such as diagnosis, treatment, and patient monitoring.

Machine learning-based systems: Machine learning-based systems use algorithms that can learn from data to provide recommendations to healthcare providers. These systems can identify patterns in patient data and making predictions based on those patterns. They can be used to support clinical decision-making in a variety of contexts, such as predicting patient outcomes, identifying high-risk patients, and optimizing treatment plans.

Natural language processing-based systems: Natural language processing-based systems use algorithms that can understand and interpret human language to provide recommendations to healthcare providers. These systems can be used to support clinical decision-making in a variety of contexts, such as reviewing patient notes, extracting data from medical records, and identifying potential drug interactions.

Applications of Clinical Decision Support Systems

CDSS have a wide range of applications in healthcare, including:

Diagnosis: CDSS can assist healthcare providers in making accurate and timely diagnoses by analyzing patient data and providing recommendations based on established guidelines and best practices.

Treatment: CDSS can assist healthcare providers in selecting appropriate treatments for patients by analyzing patient data and providing recommendations based on established guidelines and best practices.

Patient monitoring: CDSS can assist healthcare providers in monitoring patients and identifying potential complications or adverse events by analyzing patient data and providing recommendations based on established guidelines and best practices.

Disease management: CDSS can assist healthcare providers in managing chronic diseases by analyzing patient data and providing recommendations for treatment plans, lifestyle changes, and self-management strategies.

Benefits of Clinical Decision Support Systems

The use of CDSS has several potential benefits, including:

Improved patient outcomes: CDSS can assist healthcare providers in making more accurate and timely diagnoses, selecting appropriate treatments, and monitoring patients, which can lead to improved patient outcomes.

Reduced medical errors: CDSS can assist healthcare providers in avoiding errors, such as misdiagnosis, medication errors, and adverse events, which can lead to improved patient safety.

Increased efficiency: CDSS can assist healthcare providers in making more efficient use of their time by automating routine tasks, such as data analysis and report generation, and by providing timely and relevant information to support clinical decision-making.

Cost savings: CDSS can assist healthcare providers in reducing the costs associated with healthcare delivery by avoiding unnecessary tests, procedures, and treatments, and by identifying cost-effective treatment options.

Challenges of Clinical Decision Support Systems

The use of CDSS also presents several challenges, including:
Data quality and availability: CDSS rely on high-quality and comprehensive patient data to make accurate recommendations. However, data quality and availability can be a challenge in healthcare, particularly in settings where electronic health records are not widely adopted or interoperable.

Integration with existing systems: CDSS need to be integrated with existing healthcare systems, such as electronic health records and clinical workflows, to be effective. However, integration can be challenging, as healthcare systems are often complex and heterogeneous, and may use different data formats and standards.

User acceptance and adoption: CDSS can be complex and may require changes to clinical workflows and practices. User acceptance and adoption can be a challenge, particularly if healthcare providers perceive CDSS as adding to their workload or interfering with their clinical judgment.

Liability and legal issues: CDSS can introduce liability and legal issues, particularly if they provide incorrect or inappropriate recommendations that lead to adverse patient outcomes. There may also be concerns around patient privacy and data security.

____ of Clinical Decision Support Systems

There are several examples of CDSS currently in use in healthcare. Some of these include:

UpToDate: UpToDate is a knowledge-based CDSS that provides evidence-based clinical information and recommendations to healthcare providers. It covers over 11,000 clinical topics and is updated daily.

IBM Watson for Oncology: IBM Watson for Oncology is a machine learning-based CDSS that provides treatment recommendations for cancer patients. It analyzes patient data, medical literature, and other relevant sources to provide personalized treatment options.

Cerner Millennium: Cerner Millennium is a natural language processing-based CDSS that uses machine learning to extract data from medical records and provide clinical insights to healthcare providers.

Epic Deterioration Index: The Epic Deterioration Index is a machine learning-based CDSS that analyzes patient data to identify high-risk patients who may be at risk for clinical deterioration. It provides real-time alerts to healthcare providers to help prevent adverse events.

Summary: Clinical Decision Support Systems

CDSS have the potential to improve patient outcomes, reduce medical errors, and increase the efficiency of healthcare delivery. They can support clinical decision-making in a variety of contexts, such as diagnosis, treatment, patient monitoring, and disease management. However, the use of CDSS also presents several challenges, such as data quality and availability, integration with existing systems, user acceptance and adoption, and liability and legal issues.

Despite these challenges, the use of CDSS is likely to continue to grow in healthcare, as healthcare providers look for ways to improve the quality and efficiency of care. As technology continues to advance, we can expect to see more sophisticated and effective CDSS that are capable of analyzing increasingly complex and diverse patient data.

Patient Monitoring And Management

Patient monitoring and management are critical components of healthcare delivery. They involve the collection and analysis of patient data to support clinical decision-making and improve patient outcomes. Advances in technology, particularly in the areas of sensors, wearables, and data analytics, have enabled the development of innovative patient monitoring and management systems that can support a range of clinical applications.

In this section, we'll discuss the different types of patient monitoring and management systems, their applications in healthcare, and the challenges associated with their implementation and adoption.

Types of Patient Monitoring and Management Systems

There are several types of patient monitoring and management systems that are currently in use in healthcare. Some of these include:

Remote Patient Monitoring: Remote patient monitoring (RPM) involves the use of sensors and wearables to collect patient data outside of traditional clinical settings. This data can include vital signs, activity levels, medication adherence, and other health-related metrics. RPM can enable healthcare providers to monitor patients in real-time and provide timely interventions if needed.

Clinical Decision Support Systems (CDSS): As discussed in the previous section, CDSS can also be used for patient monitoring and management. They can analyze patient data and provide real-time alerts to healthcare providers if a patient's condition deteriorates or if there is a risk of an adverse event.

Electronic Health Records (EHRs): EHRs are digital records of a patient's health history and current health status. They can be used to track patient data over time and provide insights into a patient's health trends and risks.

Patient Portals: Patient portals are web-based applications that allow patients to access their health information, communicate with their healthcare providers, and manage their health. They can be used to support patient self-management and improve patient engagement in their care.

Applications of Patient Monitoring and Management Systems

Patient monitoring and management systems have a range of applications in healthcare. Some of these include:

Chronic Disease Management: RPM can be used to monitor patients with chronic diseases such as diabetes, heart disease, and COPD. By collecting patient data in real-time, healthcare providers can identify early warning signs of a disease exacerbation and provide timely interventions to prevent hospitalization or other adverse outcomes.

Post-Operative Monitoring: RPM can also be used to monitor patients after surgery. By collecting patient data such as vital signs, pain levels, and medication adherence, healthcare providers can identify potential complications and provide timely interventions to prevent readmissions or other adverse events.

Patient Engagement: Patient portals can be used to support patient engagement in their care. Patients can access their health information, communicate with their healthcare providers, and manage their health goals and plans. This can improve patient satisfaction and adherence to treatment regimens.

Clinical Decision-Making: CDSS can be used to support clinical decision-making in a range of contexts, such as patient diagnosis, treatment planning, and disease management. By analyzing patient data in real-time, CDSS can provide healthcare providers with timely and relevant information to inform their clinical decisions.

Challenges of Patient Monitoring and Management Systems

Despite the potential benefits of patient monitoring and management systems, there are several challenges associated with their implementation and adoption. Some of these include:

Data Quality and Standardization: Patient data collected from different sources can be heterogeneous and may use different data formats and standards. This can make it difficult to integrate data from multiple sources and analyze it effectively.

Privacy and Security: Patient data collected from RPM and patient portals must be protected to ensure patient privacy and data security. Healthcare providers must ensure that patient data is collected and transmitted securely, and that patient consent is obtained for data collection and use.

User Acceptance and Adoption: Patient monitoring and

management systems can be complex and may require changes to clinical workflows and processes. Healthcare providers may be resistant to adopting new technologies and may require additional training and support to effectively use these systems. Addressing these challenges requires a coordinated effort from healthcare providers, technology vendors, and regulatory agencies. It also requires a commitment to continuous improvement and innovation in patient monitoring and management systems.

Cost and Sustainability: Patient monitoring and management systems can be expensive to implement and maintain. Healthcare organizations must consider the cost-benefit of these systems and ensure that they are sustainable over the long-term.

Regulatory Compliance: Patient monitoring and management systems must comply with regulatory requirements, such as HIPAA, to ensure patient privacy and data security.

Future of Patient Monitoring and Management

The future of patient monitoring and management is likely to be driven by advances in technology, such as the Internet of Things (IoT), artificial intelligence (AI), and machine learning (ML). These technologies can enable more comprehensive and personalized patient monitoring and management, leading to improved patient outcomes and more efficient healthcare delivery.

Some future directions for patient monitoring and management include:

Predictive Analytics: Predictive analytics can be used to identify patients at risk of adverse events, such as hospitalization or disease exacerbation. By analyzing patient data over time, predictive analytics can identify patterns and trends that can inform clinical decision-making and support proactive interventions.

Wearable Technology: Wearable technology, such as smartwatches and fitness trackers, can enable more continuous and real-time patient monitoring. These devices can collect data on vital signs, activity levels, and other health-related metrics and transmit this data to healthcare providers in real-time.

Personalized Medicine: Patient monitoring and management systems can be used to support personalized medicine, which involves tailoring treatment regimens to individual patients based on their unique health characteristics and needs. By collecting and analyzing patient data over time, healthcare providers can identify patterns and trends that can inform personalized treatment plans.

Integration with EHRs: Patient monitoring and management systems can be integrated with EHRs to enable more comprehensive patient data collection and analysis. This can improve the accuracy and completeness of patient data and support more informed clinical decision-making.

Summary: Patient Monitoring and Management

Patient monitoring and management systems are critical components of healthcare delivery. They enable healthcare providers to collect and analyze patient data in real-time and support clinical decision-making to improve patient outcomes. Advances in technology, particularly in the areas of sensors, wearables, and data analytics, have enabled the development of innovative patient monitoring and management systems that can support a range of clinical applications. However, the implementation and adoption of these systems can be challenging, requiring a coordinated effort from healthcare providers, technology vendors, and regulatory agencies. The future of patient monitoring and management is likely to be driven by advances in technology, with a focus on personalized medicine, predictive analytics, and integration with EHRs.

Healthcare Operations And Resource Optimization

Healthcare operations and resource optimization are critical components of delivering high-quality and cost-effective healthcare services. Healthcare providers face a range of challenges in managing their operations, including resource constraints, fluctuating demand, and the need to maintain high levels of quality and patient satisfaction. Advances in technology, particularly in the areas of data analytics, machine learning, and artificial intelligence, are enabling healthcare providers to optimize their operations and resources more effectively, leading to improved patient outcomes and increased operational efficiency.

This section provide an overview of healthcare operations and resource optimization and discuss some of the key challenges facing healthcare providers. We will also explore some of the technologies and strategies that healthcare providers can use to optimize their operations and resources and discuss some future directions in this area.

Challenges in Healthcare Operations and Resource Optimization

Healthcare providers face a range of challenges in managing their operations and resources. Some of the key challenges include:

Resource Constraints: Healthcare providers often face resource constraints, such as limited staff, equipment, and facilities.

These constraints can limit the capacity of healthcare organizations to deliver high-quality and timely care.

Fluctuating Demand: Healthcare demand is often unpredictable and can fluctuate rapidly, making it difficult for healthcare providers to plan and allocate resources effectively.

Patient Safety and Quality: Healthcare providers must maintain high levels of patient safety and quality, while also managing their operations and resources effectively.

Cost Control: Healthcare providers must manage their costs effectively to maintain financial sustainability and deliver high-value care.

Technologies and Strategies for Healthcare Operations and Resource Optimization

Healthcare providers can use a range of technologies and strategies to optimize their operations and resources, including:

Data Analytics: Data analytics can be used to collect, analyze, and interpret large volumes of data from a range of sources, including electronic health records (EHRs), financial systems, and patient satisfaction surveys. By using data analytics, healthcare providers can identify patterns and trends in their operations and resources, enabling them to optimize their processes and improve patient outcomes.

Process Optimization: Process optimization involves streamlining workflows and eliminating inefficiencies in healthcare operations. This can be achieved by using techniques such as Lean Six Sigma and Value Stream Mapping.

Patient Flow Management: Patient flow management involves managing the movement of patients through healthcare facilities to ensure timely and efficient care. This can be achieved by using techniques such as appointment scheduling, patient triage, and bed management.

Predictive Analytics: Predictive analytics involves using machine learning algorithms to identify patterns and trends in patient data and predict future outcomes. This can be used to improve resource allocation and patient outcomes.

Robotic Process Automation (RPA): RPA involves automating repetitive and routine tasks using software robots. This can free up staff time for higher-value activities and improve operational efficiency.

Telehealth: Telehealth involves delivering healthcare services remotely, using technologies such as video conferencing and remote monitoring. This can reduce the need for in-person visits and improve access to care, particularly in rural or remote areas.

Future of Healthcare Operations and Resource Optimization

The future of healthcare operations and resource optimization is likely to be driven by advances in technology and data analytics. Some future directions in this area include:

Artificial Intelligence (AI): AI involves using machine learning algorithms to analyze large volumes of data and make predictions and recommendations based on that data. AI can be used to optimize healthcare operations and resources, such as predicting patient demand and optimizing staff schedules.

Blockchain: Blockchain technology involves creating a secure and decentralized ledger of healthcare transactions. This can enable more secure and efficient healthcare transactions, such as electronic health records (EHRs) and medical billing.

Internet of Things (IoT): IoT involves connecting devices and sensors to the internet, enabling real-time data collection and analysis. IoT can be used in healthcare to monitor patient vital signs, track medication adherence, and manage medical devices.

Precision Medicine: Precision medicine involves tailoring medical treatment to individual patients based on their genetic and other characteristics. This can improve treatment outcomes and reduce healthcare costs by targeting treatments to those most likely to benefit from them.

Population Health Management: Population health management involves managing the health of populations, rather than just individual patients. This can be achieved by using data analytics to identify high-risk populations and implementing targeted interventions to improve health outcomes.

Summary: Healthcare Operations and Resource Optimization

Healthcare operations and resource optimization are critical components of delivering high-quality and cost-effective healthcare services. Healthcare providers face a range of challenges in managing their operations, including resource constraints, fluctuating demand, and the need to maintain high levels of quality and patient satisfaction. Advances in technology, particularly in the areas of data analytics, machine learning, and artificial intelligence, are enabling healthcare providers to optimize their operations and resources more effectively, leading to improved patient outcomes and increased operational efficiency. Healthcare providers can use a range of technologies and strategies to optimize their operations and resources, including data analytics, process optimization, patient flow management, predictive analytics, robotic process automation, and telehealth. The future of healthcare operations and resource optimization is likely to be driven by advances in technology and data analytics, including artificial intelligence, blockchain, Internet of Things, precision medicine, and population health management.

Precision Medicine And Personalized Care

Precision medicine, also known as personalized medicine, is an emerging field that uses genetic and other information about an individual to tailor medical treatments to their specific needs. This approach is aimed at improving patient outcomes and reducing healthcare costs by delivering the most effective treatments to those who are most likely to benefit from them. Precision medicine is enabled by advances in genomic sequencing, bioinformatics, and data analytics, which enable researchers and healthcare providers to identify the genetic and other factors that influence disease development and progression.

Precision Medicine Applications

Precision medicine has applications in a wide range of medical fields, including oncology, cardiology, neurology, and psychiatry. Some of the key applications of precision medicine include:

Cancer Treatment: Precision medicine is transforming cancer treatment by enabling healthcare providers to identify the genetic mutations that drive cancer development and progression. This information can be used to develop targeted therapies that are tailored to the specific needs of each patient. For example, some cancer patients may have a genetic mutation that makes them more susceptible to certain drugs, while others may have mutations that make them resistant to therapies.

Cardiovascular Disease: Precision medicine is also being used to improve the diagnosis and treatment of cardiovascular disease. Genetic testing can help identify individuals who are at increased risk of developing heart disease, and targeted therapies can be used to prevent or manage the disease.

Neurological Disorders: Precision medicine is being used to improve the diagnosis and treatment of neurological disorders such as Alzheimer's disease, Parkinson's disease, and multiple sclerosis. By analyzing the genetic and other factors that contribute to these diseases, healthcare providers can develop more effective treatments that are tailored to the needs of individual patients.

Psychiatry: Precision medicine is also being used to improve the treatment of mental health disorders such as depression, anxiety, and bipolar disorder. Genetic testing can help identify individuals who are at increased risk of developing these disorders, and targeted therapies can be used to prevent or manage the disease.

Challenges of Precision Medicine

While precision medicine holds great promise for improving patient outcomes, there are also several challenges that must be overcome in order to fully realize its potential. Some of the key challenges include:

Data Quality and Privacy: Precision medicine relies on accurate and comprehensive genetic and other data about patients. However, there are concerns about the quality and privacy of this data, particularly as it relates to the sharing of data between healthcare providers and researchers.

Data Analysis: Precision medicine generates vast amounts of data that must be analyzed and interpreted to provide meaningful insights into disease development and progression.

This requires sophisticated data analytics tools and expertise, which may not be available in all healthcare settings.

Patient Access: Precision medicine requires patients to have access to genetic testing and other diagnostic tools that may not be available or affordable for all patients.

Regulatory Framework: There are also challenges related to the regulation of precision medicine, including issues around safety, efficacy, and patient privacy.

Summary: Precision Medicine and Personalized Care

Precision medicine represents a major advance in healthcare, with the potential to improve patient outcomes and reduce healthcare costs by delivering targeted, personalized treatments to those who are most likely to benefit from them. While there are challenges that must be overcome in order to fully realize the potential of precision medicine, advances in technology, data analytics, and regulatory frameworks are helping to address these challenges and move precision medicine forward. The future of precision medicine is likely to be driven by advances in genomic sequencing, artificial intelligence, and other emerging technologies that will enable healthcare providers to develop more accurate, effective, and personalized treatments for a wide range of diseases and conditions.

CHAPTER 3: PATIENT CARE WITH AI IN HEALTHCARE

This chapter focuses on the use of AI in patient care, including the improvement of patient outcomes, chronic disease management, and mental health. It also explores how AI can enhance patient engagement, experience, and palliative care. This chapter also examines the potential of AI to address healthcare disparities and the challenges in evaluating the impact of AI on patient care. The sections in this chapter provide a detailed understanding of the ways in which AI can be used to enhance patient care, and the considerations that must be taken into account to ensure that AI is used ethically and effectively in patient care.

Improving Patient Outcomes With Artificial Intelligence

Artificial Intelligence (AI) has the potential to revolutionize the healthcare industry by improving patient outcomes. The use of AI in healthcare has grown significantly in recent years and is expected to continue to do so in the future. In this chapter, we will explore how AI is improving patient outcomes in healthcare.

AI has shown great promise in improving the accuracy of diagnoses and treatment plans. One of the main benefits of AI is its ability to analyze large amounts of data quickly and accurately. This can help healthcare professionals to identify patterns and predict outcomes more effectively than traditional methods. AI can also be used to analyze medical images, such as X-rays and CT scans, to identify potential health issues that may be missed by the human eye.

Another area where AI is making a difference is in patient monitoring. By using wearable devices and sensors, AI can continuously monitor a patient's vital signs and alert healthcare professionals if there are any significant changes. This can help to identify potential health problems early, which can lead to more effective treatment and better outcomes for patients.

AI is also being used to develop personalized treatment plans for patients. By analyzing a patient's medical history, genetic information, and lifestyle factors, AI can help to identify the most effective treatment options for each individual patient. This can lead to more personalized care and better outcomes for patients.

In addition, AI is being used to improve the efficiency of healthcare systems. By automating certain tasks, such as appointment scheduling and patient record keeping, AI can help to reduce the workload of healthcare professionals and free up more time for patient care. This can lead to faster diagnosis and treatment times, as well as improved patient outcomes.

Examples of AI in Healthcare

There are already numerous examples of AI being used in

healthcare to improve patient outcomes. Here are a few examples:

Diagnosing Diseases: AI is being used to diagnose diseases such as skin cancer and diabetic retinopathy. In the case of skin cancer, AI can analyze images of moles and other skin lesions to determine whether they are cancerous or benign. In the case of diabetic retinopathy, AI can analyze images of the eye to detect signs of the condition, which can lead to blindness if left untreated.

Predicting Patient Outcomes: AI can be used to predict patient outcomes, such as the likelihood of a patient developing a certain condition or the likelihood of a patient responding to a particular treatment. This can help providers develop individualized treatment plans that are tailored to the patient's specific needs.

Monitoring Patients: AI can be used to monitor patients in real-time, allowing providers to detect potential issues before they become serious. For example, AI can be used to monitor patients with heart conditions, alerting providers if the patient's heart rate or blood pressure falls outside of a certain range.

Automating Administrative Tasks: AI can be used to automate administrative tasks, such as scheduling appointments and processing paperwork. This can free up time for healthcare providers to focus on patient care and reduce the risk of errors.

Analyzing Genomic Data: AI can be used to analyze genomic data, identifying patterns and correlations that may not be apparent to humans. This can lead to new discoveries and insights that can be used to develop new treatments and therapies.

Developing Personalized Treatment Plans: AI can be used to develop personalized treatment plans for patients based on their individual needs. This can lead to better outcomes and a reduced risk of adverse reactions to medications.

However, there are also potential challenges associated with the use of AI in healthcare. For example, there is a risk of bias in AI algorithms if they are not developed and tested properly. Additionally, there are concerns about the ethical implications of using AI in healthcare, particularly with regards to privacy and data protection.

Challenges of AI in Healthcare

While AI has tremendous potential to improve patient outcomes in healthcare, it also faces a number of challenges. Here are a few of the challenges that AI faces in healthcare:

Data Privacy and Security: One of the biggest challenges facing AI in healthcare is data privacy and security. Healthcare data is highly sensitive and must be protected from unauthorized access. This can be challenging when using AI, as the algorithms often require access to large amounts of patient data to function properly.

Bias and Fairness: Another challenge facing AI in healthcare is bias and fairness. AI algorithms can be biased based on the data that they are trained on, which can lead to unfair or inaccurate predictions. For example, an AI algorithm that is trained on data from primarily white patients may not be accurate when used with patients from other racial or ethnic backgrounds.

Interoperability: AI systems in healthcare often require data from multiple sources to function properly. However, these sources may use different data formats or be incompatible with one another, making it difficult to integrate the data.

Adoption and Implementation: Finally, one of the biggest challenges facing AI in healthcare is adoption and implementation. Healthcare providers may be hesitant to adopt new technologies, especially if they require significant changes to existing workflows or processes.

Additionally, implementing AI systems in healthcare can be complex and expensive, requiring significant investment in hardware, software, and personnel.

Overcoming Challenges and Moving Forward
While AI in healthcare faces a number of challenges, there are steps that can be taken to overcome these challenges and move the field forward. Here are a few potential solutions:

Data Privacy and Security: To address data privacy and security concerns, healthcare providers can implement strict data access policies, encrypt data, and use secure cloud-based storage solutions. Additionally, AI algorithms can be designed to work with anonymized data, reducing the risk of data breaches.

Bias and Fairness: To address bias and fairness concerns, AI algorithms can be designed to account for and mitigate potential biases in the data. Additionally, diverse datasets can be used to train AI algorithms, ensuring that they are accurate and fair across all populations.

Interoperability: To address interoperability concerns, healthcare providers can work to standardize data formats and adopt common data exchange protocols. This can make it easier to integrate data from multiple sources and ensure that AI systems are working with the most complete and accurate data possible.

Adoption and Implementation: Finally, to address adoption and implementation concerns, healthcare providers can work to educate their staff on the benefits of AI in healthcare and provide training on how to use new systems and technologies. Additionally, providers can work with AI vendors to develop systems that are easy to use and integrate with existing workflows.

In conclusion, AI has the potential to significantly improve patient outcomes in healthcare. By improving the accuracy of diagnoses and treatment plans, monitoring patients more effectively, developing personalized treatment options, and improving the efficiency of healthcare systems, AI can help to provide better care to patients. However, it is important to carefully consider the potential risks and challenges associated with the use of AI in healthcare and to ensure that it is used in a responsible and ethical manner.

Artificial Intelligence In Chronic Disease Management

Chronic diseases such as diabetes, hypertension, heart disease, and cancer are among the leading causes of death and disability worldwide. Managing chronic diseases often requires continuous monitoring of symptoms, lifestyle factors, and medical treatments, which can be time-consuming and challenging for both patients and healthcare providers. The rise of artificial intelligence (AI) technologies presents an opportunity to improve chronic disease management by enabling personalized, proactive, and efficient care.

AI applications in chronic disease management can be categorized into three main areas: disease prediction and early detection, treatment optimization, and patient engagement and education.

Disease Prediction and Early Detection

AI algorithms can analyze large datasets of patient information, including electronic health records, imaging and laboratory results, and genetic data, to identify patterns and predict the likelihood of developing a chronic disease. For example, machine learning models have been developed to predict the risk of developing diabetes or cardiovascular disease based on clinical and lifestyle factors, such as age, body mass index, blood pressure, and physical activity levels. Early detection of chronic diseases can also be facilitated by AI-powered screening tools that analyze medical images or biomarkers to detect abnormalities or signs of disease progression.

Treatment Optimization

AI can assist healthcare providers in optimizing treatment plans for chronic diseases by analyzing patient data and recommending personalized interventions. For instance, AI-powered decision support systems can analyze patient symptoms, medication regimens, and medical history to suggest the most effective treatment options or dosage adjustments. AI can also help healthcare providers to identify patients who are at risk of non-adherence to treatment plans and provide interventions to improve adherence.

Patient Engagement and Education

AI can improve patient engagement and education by providing personalized and interactive health information and coaching. Chatbots or virtual assistants can be used to answer patient questions, provide reminders and motivational messages, and encourage healthy behaviors. AI-powered mobile apps or wearables can monitor patient activity levels, sleep patterns, and other lifestyle factors and provide feedback and recommendations for improving health behaviors.

Challenges and Opportunities

Despite the potential benefits of AI in chronic disease management, several challenges must be addressed to ensure its successful implementation. One key challenge is the need for high-quality and standardized data to train AI algorithms effectively. Another challenge is the need for transparent and ethical AI algorithms that do not perpetuate biases or discrimination. Additionally, healthcare providers and patients must be educated on the benefits and limitations of AI and be willing to trust and adopt AI-powered interventions.

In conclusion, AI technologies have the potential to transform chronic disease management by providing personalized, proactive, and efficient care. To realize this potential, healthcare providers, researchers, and policymakers must work together to address the challenges and opportunities presented by AI.

Artificial Inteligence In Mental Health

Mental health is a critical aspect of overall health, and it affects one's quality of life. Unfortunately, many people suffer from mental health disorders, which are often difficult to diagnose and treat. Traditional approaches to mental health treatment have relied heavily on subjective assessments and self-reporting, which can be prone to errors and biases. However, advancements in artificial intelligence (AI) are opening up new opportunities for mental health diagnosis, treatment, and management.

AI in Mental Health Diagnosis

One of the most significant applications of AI in mental health is its potential to improve diagnosis. AI algorithms can analyze large amounts of data, including physiological data, social media activity, and electronic health records, to identify patterns that may indicate a mental health disorder. For example, a machine learning algorithm may be able to identify specific language patterns that are associated with depression or anxiety.

AI in Mental Health Treatment

AI can also be used to improve the effectiveness of mental health treatment. For instance, cognitive-behavioral therapy (CBT) is a widely used treatment for depression and anxiety. AI-powered chatbots can provide CBT-like interventions through a smartphone app or other digital platforms, making therapy more accessible and convenient for patients. These chatbots can also learn and adapt based on patients' responses to their prompts, potentially improving their effectiveness.

AI in Mental Health Management

Another application of AI in mental health is in the management of mental health disorders. AI-powered chatbots can provide continuous support to patients, helping them to monitor their mood and symptoms and providing guidance when needed. AI can also be used to develop personalized treatment plans that are tailored to a patient's specific needs and preferences.

Challenges and Considerations

While the potential benefits of AI in mental health are promising, there are also several challenges and considerations that must be addressed. First, there are concerns about privacy and data security, particularly when sensitive patient information is being collected and analyzed. Additionally, there is a risk of algorithmic bias, where AI models may inadvertently reinforce existing biases or discrimination. Finally, AI should not be seen as a replacement for human therapists, but rather as a tool to augment and support mental health treatment.

In conclusion, AI has the potential to revolutionize the field of mental health, offering new opportunities for diagnosis, treatment, and management. As AI continues to evolve, it is essential that researchers, clinicians, and policymakers work together to ensure that its applications are ethical, transparent, and equitable. Ultimately, the goal of AI in mental health should be to improve patient outcomes and quality of life, while also respecting patient privacy and autonomy.

Artificial Intelligence And Patient Engagement

Patient engagement is a critical component of healthcare, as engaged patients tend to have better health outcomes and higher levels of satisfaction with their care. However, engaging patients can be challenging, as patients often face barriers to accessing healthcare services and may not fully understand their health conditions. Artificial intelligence (AI) has the potential to improve patient engagement by providing personalized, timely, and actionable information to patients.

AI-Powered Chatbots

One of the most promising applications of AI in patient engagement is the use of AI-powered chatbots. Chatbots can be programmed to provide patients with information about their health conditions, medications, and treatment plans. They can also answer questions about symptoms and provide advice on when to seek medical attention. Chatbots can be accessed through various platforms, such as smartphone apps, messaging services, and websites, making them highly accessible to patients.

Personalized Recommendations

AI can also be used to provide personalized recommendations to patients. By analyzing patient data, such as medical records, vital signs, and lifestyle behaviors, AI algorithms can identify patterns that may be associated with certain health conditions. Based on these patterns, AI can recommend personalized interventions, such as changes in diet or exercise, to help patients manage their health.

Remote Monitoring

AI can also be used to remotely monitor patients, which can be particularly helpful for patients with chronic conditions. Remote monitoring can help patients stay on top of their health by tracking their symptoms, vital signs, and medication adherence. If any issues arise, AI can alert healthcare providers to intervene, potentially preventing complications or hospitalizations.

Challenges and Considerations

While the potential benefits of AI in patient engagement are promising, there are also several challenges and considerations that must be addressed. First, there is a risk of overreliance on AI, which could lead to patients neglecting important aspects of their health, such as seeking medical attention when necessary. Additionally, there are concerns about privacy and data security, particularly when sensitive patient information is being collected and analyzed. Finally, it is important to ensure that AI interventions are accessible to all patients, regardless of their socioeconomic status or technological literacy.

In conclusion, AI has the potential to transform patient engagement by providing personalized, timely, and actionable information to patients. As AI continues to evolve, it is essential that researchers, clinicians, and policymakers work together to ensure that its applications are ethical, transparent, and equitable. Ultimately, the goal of AI in patient engagement should be to improve patient outcomes and quality of life, while also respecting patient privacy and autonomy.

Enhancing The Patient Experience With Artificial Intelligence

The patient experience is a critical component of healthcare, as patients who have positive experiences tend to have better health outcomes and higher levels of satisfaction with their care. However, providing a positive patient experience can be challenging, as patients often face long wait times, confusing medical jargon, and limited access to healthcare services. Artificial intelligence (AI) has the potential to improve the patient experience by providing personalized, streamlined, and efficient care.

Virtual Assistants

One of the most promising applications of AI in enhancing the patient experience is the use of virtual assistants. Virtual assistants can be programmed to answer patient questions, provide information about medical conditions and treatment options, and help patients schedule appointments or refill prescriptions. By providing patients with a 24/7 resource for healthcare information and assistance, virtual assistants can improve patient satisfaction and reduce the burden on healthcare providers.

Predictive Analytics

AI can also be used to provide predictive analytics, which can help healthcare providers anticipate and prevent potential issues before they occur. For example, predictive analytics can help healthcare providers identify patients who are at risk of readmission, allowing them to intervene with appropriate care and support to prevent future hospitalizations. By identifying potential issues before they escalate, predictive analytics can improve patient outcomes and reduce healthcare costs.

Patient Monitoring

AI can also be used to monitor patients remotely, providing real-time updates on patient health and alerting healthcare providers to potential issues. For example, AI can monitor patient vital signs and detect changes that may indicate a potential health problem, such as an infection or cardiac event. By providing timely alerts to healthcare providers, AI can help prevent complications and improve patient outcomes.

Challenges and Considerations

While the potential benefits of AI in enhancing the patient experience are promising, there are also several challenges and considerations that must be addressed. First, there is a risk of overreliance on AI, which could lead to patients feeling disconnected from their healthcare providers. Additionally, there are concerns about privacy and data security, particularly when sensitive patient information is being collected and analyzed. Finally, it is important to ensure that AI interventions are accessible to all patients, regardless of their socioeconomic status or technological literacy.

In conclusion, AI has the potential to transform the patient experience by providing personalized, streamlined, and efficient care. As AI continues to evolve, it is essential that researchers, clinicians, and policymakers work together to ensure that its applications are ethical, transparent, and equitable. Ultimately, the goal of AI in enhancing the patient experience should be to improve patient outcomes and quality of life, while also respecting patient privacy and autonomy. By leveraging the power of AI, healthcare providers can provide better care and a more positive experience for patients.

Artificial Intelligence And Palliative Care

Palliative care is a specialized type of care that aims to improve the quality of life for patients with serious illnesses. Palliative care focuses on managing symptoms, providing emotional support, and helping patients make informed decisions about their care. Artificial intelligence (AI) has the potential to enhance palliative care by providing personalized and timely support to patients and their families.

Predictive Analytics

AI can be used to provide predictive analytics in palliative care, helping healthcare providers identify patients who may be approaching the end of their lives. By analyzing patient data, such as medical history, vital signs, and symptom progression, AI algorithms can identify patterns that may indicate a decline in health. This information can help healthcare providers tailor care plans and support to individual patients, ensuring that they receive the care they need at the appropriate time.

Personalized Care Plans

AI can also be used to develop personalized care plans for patients in palliative care. By analyzing patient data, AI algorithms can identify patterns that may be associated with certain symptoms or complications. Based on this information, AI can recommend personalized interventions to help manage symptoms and improve patient comfort. Additionally, AI can provide real-time updates on patient symptoms and alert healthcare providers to potential issues, enabling them to intervene promptly and provide appropriate care.

Emotional Support

Palliative care is not just about managing physical symptoms; it also involves providing emotional support to patients and their families. AI can be used to provide emotional support by analyzing patient data and providing personalized recommendations for emotional support resources. For example, AI algorithms can recommend support groups, counseling services, or meditation exercises based on a patient's individual needs and preferences.

Challenges and Considerations

While the potential benefits of AI in palliative care are promising, there are also several challenges and considerations that must be addressed. First, there is a risk of overreliance on AI, which could lead to patients feeling disconnected from their healthcare providers. Additionally, there are concerns about privacy and data security, particularly when sensitive patient information is being collected and analyzed. Finally, it is important to ensure that AI interventions are accessible to all patients, regardless of their socioeconomic status or technological literacy.

In conclusion, AI has the potential to transform palliative care by providing personalized and timely support to patients and their families. As AI continues to evolve, it is essential that researchers, clinicians, and policymakers work together to ensure that its applications are ethical, transparent, and equitable. Ultimately, the goal of AI in palliative care should be to improve patient outcomes and quality of life, while also respecting patient privacy and autonomy. By leveraging the power of AI, healthcare providers can provide better care and support to patients and their families during a challenging time.

Artificial Intelligence And Healthcare Disparities

Healthcare disparities refer to differences in health outcomes and access to healthcare services among different populations. Healthcare disparities can be caused by a variety of factors, including socioeconomic status, race, ethnicity, and geographic location. Artificial intelligence (AI) has the potential to help address healthcare disparities by providing more equitable and accessible healthcare services.

Identifying Disparities

AI can be used to identify healthcare disparities by analyzing large amounts of data from electronic health records (EHRs). By analyzing patient data, AI algorithms can identify patterns and trends that may indicate disparities in healthcare access and outcomes. For example, AI can identify disparities in screening rates for certain medical conditions, such as breast cancer or colon cancer, and help healthcare providers develop targeted interventions to improve screening rates among underrepresented populations.

Improving Access

AI can also be used to improve access to healthcare services for underserved populations. For example, telemedicine platforms that use AI can provide remote consultations and monitoring for patients who live in rural or low-income areas. Additionally, AI can be used to develop targeted outreach programs to increase awareness of healthcare services among underserved populations.

Reducing Bias

One of the challenges in addressing healthcare disparities is the presence of bias in healthcare delivery. AI can help reduce bias by standardizing healthcare protocols and removing subjective decision-making. Additionally, AI algorithms can be trained to recognize and correct for biases in patient data, ensuring that all patients receive the same level of care regardless of their demographic characteristics.

Challenges and Considerations

While the potential benefits of AI in addressing healthcare disparities are promising, there are also several challenges and considerations that must be addressed. First, there is a risk of perpetuating biases in AI algorithms if the data used to train the algorithms are not representative of the entire population. Additionally, there are concerns about privacy and data security, particularly when sensitive patient information is being collected and analyzed. Finally, it is important to ensure that AI interventions are accessible to all patients, regardless of their socioeconomic status or technological literacy.

In conclusion, AI has the potential to help address healthcare disparities by identifying disparities, improving access to healthcare services, and reducing bias in healthcare delivery. As AI continues to evolve, it is essential that researchers, clinicians, and policymakers work together to ensure that its applications are ethical, transparent, and equitable. Ultimately, the goal of AI in healthcare should be to improve health outcomes and access to care for all patients, regardless of their demographic characteristics. By leveraging the power of AI, healthcare providers can work to address healthcare disparities and provide more equitable and accessible healthcare services to all patients.

Evaluating The Impact Of Artificial Intelligence On Patient Care

The use of artificial intelligence (AI) in healthcare has the potential to revolutionize patient care by improving accuracy, efficiency, and access to care. However, it is essential to evaluate the impact of AI on patient care to ensure that its benefits outweigh its risks and challenges.

Measuring Success

Measuring the impact of AI on patient care requires a comprehensive approach that considers both clinical and non-clinical outcomes. Clinical outcomes include improvements in patient health outcomes, such as reduced mortality rates or improved disease management. Non-clinical outcomes include improvements in healthcare delivery, such as reduced wait times or increased patient satisfaction.

Data Collection and Analysis

To evaluate the impact of AI on patient care, data collection and analysis are essential. Data can be collected from a variety of sources, including electronic health records (EHRs), patient surveys, and clinical trials. This data can then be analyzed using statistical methods to identify patterns and trends.

Ethical Considerations

As with any healthcare intervention, there are ethical considerations to consider when evaluating the impact of AI on patient care. It is important to ensure that the use of AI is consistent with ethical principles, such as respect for patient autonomy, beneficence, and non-maleficence. Additionally, it is important to ensure that the use of AI does not perpetuate healthcare disparities or violate patient privacy.

Challenges and Considerations

There are several challenges and considerations to consider when evaluating the impact of AI on patient care. One challenge is the need for high-quality data that accurately reflects patient outcomes and experiences. Additionally, there is a risk of overreliance on AI, which could lead to patients feeling disconnected from their healthcare providers. Finally, there are concerns about the potential for AI to perpetuate biases or reinforce existing healthcare disparities.

In conclusion, evaluating the impact of AI on patient care is essential to ensure that its benefits outweigh its risks and challenges. Measuring both clinical and non-clinical outcomes, collecting and analyzing data, and considering ethical principles are all essential components of evaluating the impact of AI on patient care. By carefully evaluating the impact of AI on patient care, healthcare providers can work to ensure that its applications are ethical, transparent, and equitable, and ultimately improve patient outcomes and access to care.

CHAPTER 4:
FINANCIAL
MANAGEMENT WITH
AI IN HEALTHCARE

T his chapter focuses on the use of AI in predicting billing and financial management in healthcare. It explores the role of AI in billing and revenue cycle management, the various applications of AI in healthcare financial management, and how AI can be used to detect fraud. This chapter also discusses the benefits and challenges of AI in healthcare financial management and offers insights into implementing AI in billing and financial management in healthcare. The sections in this chapter provide a detailed understanding of how AI can be leveraged to improve financial management in healthcare and the considerations that must be taken into account to ensure that AI is used effectively.

The Role Of Artificial Intelligence In Billing And Revenue Cycle Management

In recent years, the healthcare industry has seen a significant increase in the use of artificial intelligence (AI) to improve patient care and operational efficiency. One area where AI has shown particular promise is in billing and revenue cycle management. Accurate billing and timely collection of payments are essential to maintaining financial stability and ensuring the quality of patient care. AI can help healthcare organizations improve billing and revenue cycle management by streamlining processes, reducing errors, and enhancing revenue capture.

Goals of AI in Healthcare Financial Management

Automating Routine Tasks: One way AI can improve billing and revenue cycle management is by automating many of the routine tasks involved in the process. For example, AI can be used to automatically assign billing codes to medical procedures, which can reduce errors and improve accuracy. AI can also automate claim submission, payment processing, and denial management, freeing up staff to focus on more complex tasks.

Reducing Errors: AI can also help identify and resolve errors and discrepancies in the billing and revenue cycle management process. For example, AI can analyze claims data to identify patterns that may indicate fraudulent billing or other irregularities. AI can also analyze denied claims to identify common reasons for denial, such as incomplete or inaccurate information, and provide suggestions for resolving these issues.

Enhancing Revenue Capture: By improving accuracy and reducing errors, AI can help healthcare organizations improve their revenue capture. For example, AI can analyze claims data to identify areas where the organization may be underbilling or missing opportunities to bill for services provided. By identifying these opportunities, AI can help healthcare organizations capture more revenue and improve their financial performance.

Benefits of AI in Healthcare Financial Management

Improved Efficiency: One of the main benefits of AI in healthcare financial management is improved efficiency. AI can automate repetitive tasks, such as data entry and record-keeping, freeing up staff time for more complex and strategic tasks. AI can also speed up financial processes, such as claims processing and reimbursement, by identifying errors and processing claims more quickly.

Increased Accuracy: AI can improve the accuracy of financial management by analyzing large amounts of data to identify patterns and trends that may not be apparent to human analysts. AI algorithms can detect errors and inconsistencies in financial data, reducing the likelihood of errors in billing, claims processing, and reimbursement.

Better Decision-Making: AI can provide healthcare organizations with more accurate and timely information to support decision-making. For example, AI can be used to develop predictive models that identify high-risk patients, enabling healthcare organizations to intervene and prevent costly medical complications before they occur.

Cost Savings: By improving efficiency, accuracy, and decision-making, AI can help healthcare organizations save money. AI can help identify areas of waste and inefficiency, reduce errors and inconsistencies, and streamline processes, resulting in significant cost savings over time.

Challenges of AI in Healthcare Financial Management

Data Quality: One of the main challenges of using AI in healthcare financial management is ensuring data quality. Healthcare data is often fragmented and stored in disparate systems, which can make it difficult to integrate and analyze. Data quality issues, such as incomplete or inaccurate data, can compromise the accuracy of AI algorithms and lead to incorrect decisions.

Data Security and Privacy: Another challenge of using AI in healthcare financial management is ensuring data security and privacy. Healthcare organizations must ensure that patient data is protected and compliant with regulatory requirements, such as HIPAA. Healthcare organizations must also protect their own financial data from cyber threats.

Expertise: Healthcare organizations must have the necessary expertise to develop and implement AI algorithms and interpret the results. This requires a skilled workforce with expertise in data science, machine learning, and analytics. Hiring and training employees with these skills can be challenging and expensive.

Integration with Existing Systems: Integrating AI with existing financial management systems can be challenging. Healthcare organizations must ensure that AI algorithms are compatible with existing systems and can be integrated without disrupting existing workflows. This requires careful planning and coordination to ensure a smooth implementation.

Applications In Healthcare Financial Management

Healthcare financial management is a complex and multifaceted process that involves managing revenue, expenses, and regulatory compliance. The use of artificial intelligence (AI) in healthcare financial management has the potential to streamline processes, reduce costs, and improve decision-making. In this section, we will explore some of the key applications of AI in healthcare financial management.

Revenue Cycle Management

Revenue cycle management is the process of managing the financial interactions between a healthcare provider and patients, payers, and regulatory bodies. AI can be used to improve revenue cycle management by automating processes, reducing errors, and improving efficiency. For example, AI can be used to automate the billing and claims process, analyze claims data to identify trends, and optimize pricing strategies to improve revenue capture.

Financial Planning and Analysis

AI can also be used in financial planning and analysis to improve forecasting accuracy and identify areas of opportunity for cost savings. By analyzing large datasets, AI algorithms can identify patterns and trends that may not be apparent to human analysts. This can help healthcare organizations make more informed financial decisions and optimize their operations to reduce costs.

Fraud Detection and Prevention

Healthcare fraud is a significant problem that costs the industry billions of dollars each year. AI can be used to detect and prevent healthcare fraud by analyzing claims data to identify patterns that may indicate fraudulent activity. AI can also be used to monitor transactions in real-time and flag any suspicious activity for further investigation.

Risk Management

Risk management is an essential component of healthcare financial management, and AI can be used to improve risk management strategies. For example, AI algorithms can analyze claims data to identify high-risk patients and develop personalized care plans to mitigate their risk. AI can also be used to optimize insurance coverage and pricing strategies to reduce risk and improve financial performance.

Artificial Intelligence And Fraud Detection In Healthcare

Healthcare fraud is a significant problem that costs the industry billions of dollars each year. Fraudulent activity can take many forms, including billing for services that were not provided, billing for services that were medically unnecessary, and submitting false claims to insurance providers. The detection and prevention of healthcare fraud are essential components of healthcare financial management. The use of artificial intelligence (AI) in fraud detection has the potential to improve the accuracy and efficiency of these efforts. In this section, we will explore the role of AI in healthcare fraud detection.

What is Healthcare Fraud?

Healthcare fraud is the intentional deception or misrepresentation of information that results in an unauthorized benefit to an individual or entity. Healthcare fraud can be committed by healthcare providers, patients, and insurance companies. Some common types of healthcare fraud include billing for services not rendered, not medically necessary, a more expensive service than was actually provided and accepting or offering bribes for referrals or services

The Role of AI in Fraud Detection

AI can be used to detect and prevent healthcare fraud by analyzing large datasets to identify patterns that may indicate fraudulent activity. AI algorithms can analyze claims data, electronic health records, and other data sources to identify unusual billing patterns, identify high-risk patients, and monitor transactions in real-time for suspicious activity.

One of the key advantages of AI in fraud detection is its ability to analyze large datasets quickly and accurately. AI algorithms can identify patterns and trends that may not be apparent to human analysts, and can flag any suspicious activity for further investigation. This can help healthcare organizations detect and prevent fraud more quickly and accurately than traditional methods.

AI can also be used to develop predictive models that can identify high-risk patients or providers. For example, AI algorithms can analyze claims data to identify patients who have a history of submitting fraudulent claims, or providers who have a history of overbilling or other fraudulent activity. By identifying high-risk individuals, healthcare organizations can develop targeted interventions to prevent fraud before it occurs.

Challenges of Implementing AI in Fraud Detection

While AI has significant potential to improve healthcare fraud detection, there are also challenges associated with implementing this technology. One of the biggest challenges is the lack of standardization in healthcare data. Healthcare data is often fragmented and stored in disparate systems, which can make it difficult to integrate and analyze. Another challenge is the need for expertise in data science and analytics. Healthcare organizations must have the necessary expertise to develop and implement AI algorithms and interpret the results.

In conclusion, AI has significant potential to improve healthcare fraud detection by analyzing large datasets to identify patterns and trends that may indicate fraudulent activity. By flagging suspicious activity for further investigation, AI can help healthcare organizations detect and prevent fraud more quickly and accurately than traditional methods. However, implementing AI in healthcare fraud detection requires careful planning and consideration of the benefits and challenges associated with this technology. Healthcare organizations must develop a strategic plan for implementing AI and ensure they have the necessary expertise and infrastructure to support this technology.

Implementing Artificial Intelligence In Billing And Financial Management

Implementing AI in billing and financial management in healthcare can be a complex process, but careful planning and execution can ensure success. Below are some key considerations for implementing AI in billing and financial management:

Identify Key Processes: The first step in implementing AI in billing and financial management is to identify the key processes that can benefit from automation. These may include tasks such as claims processing, payment posting, denial management, and revenue cycle management. Begin by conducting a needs assessment to identify areas where AI can be applied to improve billing and financial management. This should include a review of existing processes, systems, and data, as well as an analysis of key performance indicators.

Define Goals: It is important to clearly define the goals of implementing AI in billing and financial management. These may include reducing manual errors, improving accuracy and efficiency, reducing costs, and increasing revenue.

Select the Right AI Solution: Healthcare organizations must select the right AI solution that meets their specific needs. This may involve evaluating multiple vendors and solutions, and assessing their capabilities, scalability, and compatibility with existing systems.

Integrate AI with Existing Systems: Integration with existing financial management systems is critical for successful implementation of AI in billing and financial management. Healthcare organizations must ensure that AI solutions are compatible with existing systems and can be integrated without disrupting existing workflows.

Ensure Data Quality and Security: Healthcare organizations must ensure that data used to train AI algorithms is of high quality and compliant with privacy and security regulations, such as HIPAA. Data security measures, such as encryption and access controls, must also be implemented to protect patient and financial data.

Train Staff: AI implementation requires staff training to ensure that they can use the new tools effectively. This may involve training on the use of AI algorithms, interpreting results, and integrating AI with existing workflows.

Monitor and Evaluate Results: Healthcare organizations must continuously monitor and evaluate the performance of AI solutions to ensure that they are meeting their goals. This may involve measuring key performance indicators, such as accuracy and efficiency, and making adjustments as necessary.

Address Ethical Concerns: AI implementation must address ethical concerns related to privacy, security, and bias. Healthcare organizations must ensure that they are transparent about their use of AI and have appropriate safeguards in place to prevent harmful outcomes.

Continuously Improve: Continuously improve the AI solution and processes by incorporating feedback from staff and stakeholders and making adjustments to improve performance.

An alternative to implementing AI in-house is deploying point solutions or partnering with managed services vendors that excel in these areas.

In conclusion, implementing AI in billing and financial management in healthcare can be a complex process, but careful planning and execution can ensure success. Healthcare organizations must identify key processes, define goals, select the right AI solution, integrate with existing systems, ensure data quality and security, train staff, monitor and evaluate results, and address ethical concerns. By following these key considerations, healthcare organizations can realize the benefits of AI in billing and financial management.

CHAPTER 5: AI IN REVENUE CYCLE MANAGEMENT

T his chapter of the book focuses on the use of AI in front, middle and back revenue cycle management in healthcare. It explores the various applications of AI in front revenue cycle management, such as patient scheduling and registration, as well as the applications of AI in middle and back revenue cycle management, such as claims management and collections. The sections in this chapter provide a detailed understanding of how AI can be used to streamline revenue cycle management in healthcare and the considerations that must be taken into account to ensure that AI is used effectively in revenue cycle management.

Introduction To Front, Middle And Back Revenue Cycle Management

Revenue cycle management (RCM) is an essential aspect of healthcare operations that involves managing the financial transactions that occur from patient registration to payment collection. The revenue cycle begins when a patient schedules an appointment and ends when the healthcare provider receives payment for the services rendered.

Revenue cycle management can be divided into three primary components: front-end, middle and back-end. The front-end of the revenue cycle includes tasks such as patient registration, insurance verification, and pre-authorization for services. Mid revenue cycle mostly focuses on coding of claims   while the back-end of the revenue cycle includes tasks such as billing and collections.

The front-end of the revenue cycle is crucial because it sets the stage for the rest of the cycle. Accurate and timely patient registration, insurance verification, and pre-authorization can help ensure that services are reimbursed properly and that patients are not left with unexpected bills.

Patient registration involves gathering demographic and insurance information from the patient and creating a record in the healthcare provider's system. Insurance verification involves verifying the patient's insurance coverage and benefits to ensure that the services provided are covered by the patient's insurance plan. Pre-authorization involves obtaining approval from the insurance company before providing certain services, such as surgeries or diagnostic tests.

The middle and back-end of the revenue cycle involves tasks such as coding, billing, and collections. Coding involves translating the medical procedures and diagnoses into billing codes that can be submitted to insurance companies for reimbursement. Billing involves submitting claims to insurance companies and following up on unpaid claims. Collections involve collecting payment from patients for services that are not covered by insurance or for which the patient is responsible for a portion of the cost.

Effective revenue cycle management is essential for healthcare providers to operate efficiently and maintain financial stability. Poor revenue cycle management can result in lost revenue, increased costs, and decreased patient satisfaction. As healthcare becomes increasingly complex and reimbursement models continue to evolve, revenue cycle management will become even more critical for the success of healthcare providers.

The use of technology, such as artificial intelligence (AI), has the potential to improve the efficiency and accuracy of revenue cycle management. AI can automate many of the tasks involved in revenue cycle management, reducing the time and resources required and improving accuracy. In the following chapters, we will explore the various applications of AI in revenue cycle management and the challenges and considerations associated with adopting this technology.

The ultimate goal of revenue cycle management is to maximize revenue while minimizing costs and ensuring that patients receive the care they need. By optimizing the front-end and back-end of the revenue cycle, healthcare providers can streamline operations, reduce errors, and improve financial performance.

In addition to AI, other technologies such as electronic health records (EHRs), revenue cycle management software, and patient engagement tools can also help improve revenue cycle management. EHRs can provide real-time access to patient information, reducing the time required for patient registration and insurance verification. Revenue cycle management software can automate many of the tasks involved in coding, billing, and collections, reducing the time and resources required. Patient engagement tools can improve communication between patients and healthcare providers, reducing the likelihood of denied claims and increasing patient satisfaction.

Overall, effective revenue cycle management is essential for the financial health of healthcare providers and the delivery of high-quality patient care. By leveraging the latest technologies, healthcare providers can optimize their revenue cycle management processes, improve financial performance, and provide better care to their patients. In the following sections, we will explore the various ways in which AI can be used to improve front-end, middle and back-end revenue cycle management, as well as the challenges and considerations associated with adopting this technology.

Applications Of Artificial Intelligence In Front Revenue Cycle Management

Front revenue cycle management (RCM) is the process of managing patient-facing activities such as scheduling appointments, registering patients, verifying insurance eligibility, collecting on estimates, financial assistance and handling claims. The goal of front RCM is to ensure a smooth and efficient patient experience while maximizing revenue for healthcare providers.

In recent years, AI has emerged as a powerful tool for improving front RCM. AI technologies such as machine learning, natural language processing (NLP), and robotic process automation (RPA) can automate repetitive tasks, reduce errors, and improve the accuracy of data collection and analysis. In this section we will explore some of the applications of AI in front RCM.

Automating Patient Scheduling: One of the most time-consuming tasks in front RCM is scheduling patient appointments. AI-powered scheduling systems can automatically find the best available appointment times based on the patient's preferences, provider availability, and other factors. This can reduce wait times and improve patient satisfaction.

Streamlining Patient Registration: AI can also be used to streamline patient registration. NLP algorithms can extract key information from patient intake forms and automatically populate electronic health records (EHRs). RPA tools can automate the process of verifying patient insurance eligibility and collecting copays.

Improving Claims Management: AI-powered claims management systems can help healthcare providers identify registration errors and other issues that can lead to claim denials. Machine learning algorithms can analyze claims data to identify patterns and predict which claims are likely to be denied. This can help providers take corrective action before claims are created, reducing the risk of denials and improving cash flow.

Enhancing Patient Communication: AI-powered chatbots can be used to enhance patient communication by providing answers to common questions, scheduling appointments, and handling other routine tasks. NLP algorithms can help these chatbots understand and respond to natural language queries, improving the patient experience.

Predictive Analytics: AI-powered predictive analytics tools can be used to identify patients who are at high risk of not paying their bills. This can help providers take proactive steps to collect payment, such as offering payment plans or enrolling patients on financial assistance programs.

Fraud Detection: AI can also be used to detect fraud and abuse in front RCM. Machine learning algorithms can analyze claims data to identify patterns that may indicate fraudulent activity. This can help providers take corrective action before fraudulent claims are paid, reducing the risk of financial losses.

Applications Of Artificial Intelligence In Mid And Back Revenue Cycle Management

Mid and Back revenue cycle management (RCM) are the process of managing billing and payment activities for healthcare providers. This includes tasks such as coding claims, submitting claims to insurance companies, following up on unpaid claims, and managing patient billing and collections. It is essential to the financial health of healthcare providers, but it can be time-consuming and resource-intensive. In recent years, artificial intelligence (AI) has emerged as a powerful tool for improving back RCM. In this section we'll explore some of the applications of AI in mid and back RCM.

Automated Coding: AI can be used to automate the coding of claims, which is one of the most time-consuming tasks in mid RCM. Machine learning algorithms can analyze clinical documentation to identify the appropriate diagnosis and procedure codes, reducing the risk of errors and improving the accuracy of claims.

Claims Submission: AI can also be used to improve the process of submitting claims to insurance companies. RPA tools can automate the process of verifying patient eligibility, submitting claims, and following up on unpaid claims. This can reduce the time and resources required for claims submission and improve cash flow for healthcare providers.

Claims Denial Management: AI-powered claims denial management systems can help healthcare providers identify the root causes of claim denials and take corrective action to prevent them in the future. Machine learning algorithms can analyze claims data to identify patterns that may lead to denials, such as coding errors or missing information.

Patient Billing and Collections: AI can be used to improve the process of patient billing and collections. NLP algorithms can analyze patient statements to identify key information such as outstanding balances and due dates. AI-powered chatbots can be used to answer patient questions and aid with payment options.

Payment Processing: AI can automate payment processing, including posting payments and reconciling accounts. This can reduce errors and ensure that payments are processed quickly and accurately.

Revenue Cycle Analytics: AI can provide healthcare organizations with real-time data on their revenue cycle performance. This can help organizations identify areas for improvement and make data-driven decisions to improve financial outcomes.

Implementing Artificial Intelligence In Revenue Cycle Management

To implement AI in RCM effectively, healthcare providers should follow these steps:

Identify the areas where AI can have the most impact: Healthcare providers should assess their RCM process to identify areas where AI can be most effective, such as claims processing, billing, or payment collection.

Choose the right AI system: Healthcare providers should research different AI systems to find the one that best fits their needs, considering factors such as cost, functionality, and ease of integration.

Integrate the AI system with existing RCM systems: AI systems must be integrated with existing RCM systems to ensure that data is accurate and up-to-date.

Train staff: Healthcare providers must train their staff on how to use the AI system effectively, including how to interpret the results and make decisions based on the data.

Monitor and evaluate: Healthcare providers must monitor the AI system's performance and evaluate its effectiveness regularly. This will help to identify areas for improvement and ensure that the system continues to provide value over time.

AI has the potential to revolutionize front, mid and back RCM by automating repetitive tasks, improving data accuracy, and enhancing the patient experience. Implementing AI in revenue cycle management requires a significant investment in technology and training. However, the long-term benefits can outweigh the initial costs. By automating many of the manual processes involved in revenue cycle management, healthcare organizations can reduce errors, increase efficiency, and ultimately improve financial outcomes.

CHAPTER 6: SECURITY AND PRIVACY IN HEALTHCARE AI

As Artificial Intelligence (AI) continues to advance in healthcare, the importance of ensuring security and privacy of patient data becomes increasingly critical. Chapter 6 of this book focuses on security and privacy concerns in AI healthcare, addressing the challenges and risks associated with implementing AI in healthcare settings, and providing best practices and solutions to ensure the protection of sensitive patient data. The sections in this chapter will cover topics such as security threats and risks in AI healthcare, cybersecurity measures, data privacy and protection, legal and ethical considerations, addressing security challenges and ensuring compliance, and best practices for security and privacy in AI healthcare.

Security Threats And Risks In Healthcare Artificial Intelligence

As healthcare organizations increasingly adopt artificial intelligence (AI) technologies to improve patient care and operational efficiency, the potential for security threats and risks also increases. In this section we'll explore some of the security threats and risks that healthcare organizations should be aware of when using AI in healthcare.

Cybersecurity Threats

Healthcare organizations must be aware of the various types of cyber-attacks that can compromise the security of their AI systems and patient data. For example, malware can infect AI systems and steal or modify patient data, while ransomware can encrypt patient data and demand payment for its release. Phishing attacks can trick employees into revealing login credentials, which can be used to gain unauthorized access to AI systems and patient data.

To mitigate these threats, healthcare organizations should implement robust cybersecurity measures, such as firewalls, antivirus software, and intrusion detection systems. They should also conduct regular vulnerability assessments and penetration testing to identify and address potential security weaknesses in their AI systems.

Algorithm Bias

AI algorithms may exhibit bias based on the data they are trained on, which can result in discriminatory or unfair outcomes for certain patient populations. For example, if an AI algorithm is trained on data that is biased against certain racial or ethnic groups, it may produce inaccurate or unfair results for those groups.

To address algorithm bias, healthcare organizations should carefully evaluate and monitor their AI algorithms to ensure that they are fair and unbiased. This includes regularly testing algorithms for bias and updating them as necessary to ensure that they are producing accurate and fair results for all patient populations.

Malfunctioning AI Systems

AI systems may malfunction or produce inaccurate results, which can impact patient care and safety. For example, if an AI system that is used to diagnose medical conditions produces inaccurate results, patients may be misdiagnosed or treated incorrectly.

To mitigate the risks of malfunctioning AI systems, healthcare organizations should thoroughly test their AI systems for accuracy and reliability before deploying them in clinical settings. They should also monitor their AI systems for performance issues and take corrective action as necessary.

Insider Threats

Healthcare organizations must also be aware of the potential for insider threats, such as employees intentionally or unintentionally accessing or sharing patient data inappropriately. For example, an employee may access patient data without authorization or share patient data with unauthorized third parties.

To address insider threats, healthcare organizations should implement strict access controls and user authentication mechanisms to limit access to patient data to authorized personnel only. They should also provide regular training to employees on data security and privacy best practices to minimize the risk of accidental data breaches.

Inadequate Security Measures

Healthcare organizations must ensure that they have adequate security measures in place to protect their AI systems and patient data from security threats and risks. This includes implementing security policies and procedures, regularly updating software and hardware, and providing regular training for employees.

To ensure adequate security measures, healthcare organizations should conduct regular security assessments and audits to identify potential vulnerabilities and implement appropriate remediation measures.

Lack of Data Privacy

Healthcare organizations must ensure that patient data is collected, used, and disclosed in compliance with applicable laws and regulations related to data privacy, such as the Health Insurance Portability and Accountability Act (HIPAA) and the General Data Protection Regulation (GDPR). Failure to comply with these regulations can result in legal and financial penalties and damage to the organization's reputation.

To ensure compliance with data privacy regulations, healthcare organizations should implement appropriate policies and procedures for data collection, use, and disclosure, and provide regular training to employees on data privacy best practices. They should also regularly review and update their data privacy policies and procedures to ensure that they are in compliance with applicable regulations.

In summary, healthcare organizations must be aware of the various security threats and risks associated with using AI in healthcare and take appropriate measures to mitigate them. By implementing robust cybersecurity measures, addressing algorithm bias, ensuring reliable AI systems, addressing insider threats, implementing adequate security measures, and ensuring compliance with data privacy regulations, healthcare organizations can ensure that they are effectively managing security and privacy risks associated with AI in healthcare. It is important for healthcare organizations to have a comprehensive security and privacy program in place that covers all aspects of AI in healthcare, from data collection and use to system security and data sharing.

Healthcare organizations must also ensure that they are continuously monitoring and updating their security and privacy measures to keep up with evolving security threats and regulatory requirements. This includes regularly reviewing and updating their security policies and procedures, implementing new security technologies as needed, and providing ongoing training to employees on security and privacy best practices.

Ultimately, effective security and privacy measures are critical for maintaining patient trust and confidence in the healthcare system. By taking a proactive approach to security and privacy, healthcare organizations can ensure that they are protecting patient data and providing high-quality, safe care to their patients.

Cybersecurity Measures For Artificial Intelligence Healthcare

In the age of advanced technology, cybersecurity has become a crucial component of healthcare organizations' overall IT strategy. With the widespread adoption of artificial intelligence (AI) in healthcare, the need for effective cybersecurity measures has become even more critical. In this section we will discuss some cybersecurity measures that healthcare organizations can take to protect their AI systems and patient data from cyber threats.

Strong Passwords and User Authentication

One of the most basic and effective cybersecurity measures that healthcare organizations can implement is to require strong passwords and user authentication for all access to their AI systems. This means enforcing strict password policies that require complex passwords, regular password changes, and multi-factor authentication.

Multi-factor authentication requires users to provide two or more forms of identification to access a system, such as a password and a fingerprint scan. This provides an additional layer of security that makes it more difficult for cybercriminals to gain access to sensitive information.

Encryption

Encryption is another critical cybersecurity measure that healthcare organizations can use to protect their AI systems and patient data. Encryption involves converting sensitive data into an unreadable format that can only be accessed with a decryption key. This helps to ensure that even if data is stolen or intercepted, it cannot be read by unauthorized parties.

Encryption can be used to protect data at rest, such as stored patient records, as well as data in transit, such as data transmitted between healthcare organizations and third-party vendors.

Network Segmentation

Network segmentation is the process of dividing a network into smaller, isolated segments to reduce the risk of a security breach spreading throughout the entire network. This can be particularly important in healthcare organizations where sensitive patient data is stored on the same network as less sensitive data.

By segmenting the network, healthcare organizations can

isolate sensitive data and limit access to it, reducing the risk of a data breach. This can also make it easier to detect and respond to a security breach if one does occur.

Firewall

A firewall is a network security system that monitors and controls incoming and outgoing network traffic based on predetermined security rules. It acts as a barrier between the healthcare organization's internal network and the internet, preventing unauthorized access to the network.

Firewalls can be used to block malicious traffic and prevent cybercriminals from accessing sensitive patient data. They can also be used to restrict access to certain websites and applications, further reducing the risk of a security breach.

Intrusion Detection and Prevention

Intrusion detection and prevention systems (IDPS) are cybersecurity tools that monitor network traffic for signs of a security breach. IDPS can detect and alert healthcare organizations to potential threats, such as malware or unauthorized access attempts.

IDPS can also be configured to automatically respond to a potential threat by blocking the traffic or alerting security personnel. This can help healthcare organizations quickly respond to a security breach and limit the damage caused by the breach.

Regular Updates and Patches

Regular updates and patches are critical for maintaining the security of healthcare organizations' AI systems. These updates and patches typically address security vulnerabilities and fix bugs that could be exploited by cybercriminals.

Healthcare organizations should have a patch management process in place that ensures that all software and systems are regularly updated with the latest security patches. This can help to prevent cybercriminals from exploiting known vulnerabilities to gain unauthorized access to patient data.

Employee Training and Awareness

Employee training and awareness are critical components of any effective cybersecurity program. Healthcare organizations must provide regular training to employees on security best practices, including how to recognize and respond to potential security threats.

Employees should be trained on how to handle sensitive patient data and how to report any suspicious activity or security incidents. Regular security awareness training can help to reduce the risk of human error and minimize the impact of a security breach.

Incident Response Plan

Even with the most effective cybersecurity measures in place, there is always a risk of a security breach occurring. Healthcare organizations should have an incident response plan (IRP) in place that outlines the steps to be taken in the event of a security breach.

The IRP should include procedures for detecting and reporting a security breach, assessing the extent of the breach, containing the breach, and recovering from the breach. The plan should also identify the roles and responsibilities of key personnel involved in the incident response process.

Regular testing and updating of the IRP is important to ensure that it remains effective and up-to-date with changing cybersecurity threats and regulatory requirements.

Vendor Management

Healthcare organizations often work with third-party vendors, such as cloud service providers or software vendors, to provide AI solutions. These vendors may have access to sensitive patient data, making it important for healthcare organizations to have a vendor management program in place.

Vendor management should include due diligence and risk assessment of third-party vendors, as well as contractual provisions that require vendors to comply with healthcare organizations' security and privacy requirements.

Continuous Monitoring and Threat Intelligence

Continuous monitoring and threat intelligence are critical for identifying and responding to potential security threats in real-time. Healthcare organizations should use security tools that provide continuous monitoring of their AI systems and network traffic.

Threat intelligence involves collecting and analyzing data about potential security threats to identify patterns and trends. This can help healthcare organizations stay ahead of emerging cybersecurity threats and implement proactive measures to protect their AI systems and patient data.

In conclusion, healthcare organizations must take proactive steps to protect their AI systems and patient data from cyber threats. This includes implementing strong passwords and user authentication, encryption, network segmentation, firewalls, intrusion detection and prevention, regular updates and patches, employee training and awareness, incident response planning, vendor management, and continuous monitoring and threat intelligence.

By following these cybersecurity measures, healthcare organizations can help to ensure the privacy and security of patient data while providing high-quality, safe care to their patients.

Data Privacy And Protection In Artificial Intelligence Healthcare

The use of artificial intelligence (AI) in healthcare has the potential to improve patient outcomes and reduce healthcare costs. However, with the increasing use of AI comes the need for effective data privacy and protection measures. In this chapter, we will discuss the importance of data privacy and protection in AI healthcare, the risks associated with data breaches, and best practices for ensuring data privacy and protection.

Importance of Data Privacy and Protection in AI Healthcare

The use of AI in healthcare generates large amounts of data, including patient data, that must be handled with care to ensure patient privacy and confidentiality. Patients have a right to expect that their personal information will be protected, and failure to do so can result in damage to a patient's reputation, financial loss, and even identity theft.

Data breaches can also result in legal and regulatory consequences, including fines and penalties for violating privacy laws such as the Health Insurance Portability and Accountability Act (HIPAA) and the General Data Protection Regulation (GDPR).

Risks Associated with Data Breaches

The risks associated with data breaches in AI healthcare are significant. These risks include:

Unauthorized Access and Disclosure: One of the primary risks associated with data breaches is unauthorized access to and disclosure of patient data. This can occur when hackers gain access to an organization's network, or when employees or contractors inadvertently or intentionally disclose patient data.

Identity Theft: Data breaches can also result in identity theft, in which an individual's personal information is used to obtain credit, loans, or other financial benefits. This can result in financial loss and damage to an individual's credit rating.

Medical Fraud: Data breaches can also lead to medical fraud, in which an individual's medical information is used to obtain medical services or prescriptions fraudulently. This can result in financial loss and damage to an individual's medical record.

Damage to Reputation: Data breaches can also result in damage to an individual's reputation. For example, if a patient's personal and medical information is disclosed, they may be reluctant to seek medical treatment in the future, potentially resulting in negative health outcomes.

Best Practices for Ensuring Data Privacy and Protection

To ensure data privacy and protection in AI healthcare, healthcare organizations should follow these best practices:

Develop a Data Privacy and Protection Policy: Healthcare organizations should develop a data privacy and protection policy that outlines how patient data will be collected, used, and protected. This policy should be communicated to all employees and contractors, and regularly reviewed and updated to ensure compliance with changing regulatory requirements and best practices.

Conduct Risk Assessments: Healthcare organizations should conduct regular risk assessments to identify potential data privacy and protection risks and develop strategies to mitigate those risks.

Implement Access Controls: Access controls, such as passwords and two-factor authentication, should be implemented to ensure that only authorized personnel have access to patient data. Access controls should be regularly reviewed and updated to ensure that only those who need access have it.

Encrypt Data: Patient data should be encrypted both at rest and in transit to protect it from unauthorized access. Encryption keys should be securely stored and regularly rotated to ensure that data remains protected.

Implement Network Segmentation: Network segmentation can help to protect patient data by separating sensitive data from non-sensitive data. This can help to prevent unauthorized access to patient data by limiting the scope of potential data breaches.

Regularly Update and Patch Systems: Software and systems should be regularly updated and patched to address security vulnerabilities and protect against potential data breaches.

Conduct Employee Training and Awareness: Healthcare organizations should conduct regular employee training and awareness programs to ensure that employees understand their role in protecting patient data and are aware of potential data privacy and protection risks.

Monitor and Audit Access: Healthcare organizations should monitor and audit access to patient data to detect and respond to potential data breaches. This can include tracking and analyzing access logs and setting up alerts for suspicious activity.

Have a Data Breach Response Plan: Healthcare organizations should have a data breach response plan in place to ensure that they can respond quickly and effectively in the event of a data breach. This plan should include procedures for notifying patients, regulatory authorities, and other stakeholders.

Regularly Test and Evaluate Security Measures: Finally, healthcare organizations should regularly test and evaluate their data privacy and protection measures to ensure that they are effective and up to date. This can include conducting penetration testing and vulnerability assessments to identify potential weaknesses and developing strategies to address them.

Legal and Regulatory Requirements for Data Privacy and Protection

In addition to best practices, healthcare organizations must comply with legal and regulatory requirements related to data privacy and protection. The most significant of these requirements include:

HIPAA: HIPAA is a federal law that regulates the use and disclosure of patient health information (PHI). Healthcare organizations that handle PHI must comply with HIPAA regulations, which include requirements related to the protection and disclosure of PHI.

GDPR: The GDPR is a regulation that applies to organizations that process the personal data of individuals in the European Union (EU). Healthcare organizations that handle personal data of EU residents must comply with GDPR requirements, which include requirements related to data protection, security, and breach notification.

State Privacy Laws: In addition to federal laws such as HIPAA, many states have their own laws related to data privacy and protection. Healthcare organizations must comply with these laws, which can include requirements related to breach notification, data retention, and data disposal.

Cybersecurity Frameworks: Several cybersecurity frameworks have been developed to help organizations manage cybersecurity risks. One of the most widely used frameworks is the NIST Cybersecurity Framework, which provides guidelines for managing cybersecurity risks, including those related to AI systems.

FDA Guidance: The FDA has issued guidance for the regulation of medical devices that incorporate AI. Healthcare organizations that develop or use medical devices with AI components must comply with FDA regulations and guidelines.
Legal and ethical considerations related

Legal And Ethical Aspects Of Security In Artificial Intelligence

As the use of artificial intelligence (AI) in healthcare continues to grow, legal and ethical considerations related to security are becoming increasingly important. Healthcare organizations must ensure that AI systems are used in a responsible and ethical manner, while also complying with legal and regulatory requirements related to security and privacy. This section will explore the legal and ethical aspects of security in AI healthcare, including the importance of transparency, accountability, and fairness in AI systems.

Transparency in AI Healthcare

One of the key legal and ethical considerations in AI healthcare is transparency. Patients have a right to know how their data is being used and how AI systems are making decisions about their care. Healthcare organizations must be transparent about the data they collect, how it is being used, and how AI systems are making decisions based on that data.

This transparency can be achieved through various means, such as providing patients with information about the algorithms being used and the data inputs, as well as explaining how decisions are being made. In addition, healthcare organizations must ensure that patients understand the potential benefits and risks of using AI in healthcare and that they have the right to refuse AI-based care if they choose.

Accountability in AI Healthcare

Another important legal and ethical consideration in AI healthcare is accountability. Healthcare organizations must ensure that they are accountable for the decisions made by AI systems and that they can be held responsible for any harm caused by those systems. This can include establishing clear lines of responsibility and accountability, as well as developing policies and procedures for addressing potential errors or harms caused by AI systems.

One way to ensure accountability is through auditing and monitoring of AI systems. This can involve tracking the data inputs and outputs of the system, as well as the decisions made by the system. Auditing and monitoring can help identify potential errors or biases in the system and can help ensure that the system is being used in a responsible and ethical manner.

Fairness in AI Healthcare

Fairness is another critical legal and ethical consideration in AI healthcare. AI systems must be designed and implemented in a way that is fair and equitable for all patients, regardless of their race, gender, age, or other factors. This can be a challenging task, as AI systems can be susceptible to bias and may perpetuate existing disparities in healthcare.

One way to ensure fairness is by designing AI systems that are based on representative and diverse data inputs. This can help ensure that the system is not biased toward any particular patient population. In addition, healthcare organizations must regularly evaluate AI systems for bias and take steps to address any biases that are identified.

Another way to ensure fairness is through a process known as algorithmic transparency. This involves providing patients and clinicians with information about how the AI system is making decisions and what factors are being considered. Algorithmic transparency can help ensure that patients and clinicians have confidence in the decisions being made by the system and can help identify any potential biases or errors.

Ethical Considerations in Security for AI Healthcare

In addition to legal requirements, healthcare organizations must also consider ethical considerations related to security in AI healthcare. These ethical considerations can include issues related to privacy, autonomy, and beneficence.

Privacy: Privacy is a critical ethical consideration in AI healthcare. Patients have a right to privacy and confidentiality, and healthcare organizations must ensure that patient data is protected from unauthorized access, use, or disclosure. Healthcare organizations must also obtain patient consent for the use of their data in AI systems.

Autonomy: Autonomy is another important ethical consideration in AI healthcare. Patients have the right to make decisions about their care, and AI systems must be designed and implemented in a way that respects patient autonomy. Healthcare organizations must ensure that patients are informed about the use of AI in their care and that they have the right to refuse AI-based care if they choose.

Beneficence: Beneficence is the ethical principle of doing good and avoiding harm. Healthcare organizations must ensure that AI systems are used in a way that benefits patients and that they do not cause harm. This can involve regular evaluation and monitoring of AI systems to ensure that they are achieving their intended goals and that they are not causing unintended harm.

Addressing Legal and Ethical Challenges

Addressing legal and ethical challenges related to security in AI healthcare can be a complex task, but there are several best practices that healthcare organizations can follow to ensure that they are using AI systems in a responsible and ethical manner.

Conduct Regular Risk Assessments: Healthcare organizations must conduct regular risk assessments to identify potential security risks related to AI systems. These risk assessments can help identify potential vulnerabilities in the system and can help healthcare organizations develop policies and procedures to mitigate those risks.

Establish Clear Lines of Responsibility and Accountability: Healthcare organizations must establish clear lines of responsibility and accountability for AI systems. This can involve designating specific individuals or teams to oversee the implementation and use of the system and developing policies and procedures for addressing potential errors or harms caused by the system.

Ensure Algorithmic Transparency: Algorithmic transparency is critical to ensuring that AI systems are used in a fair and ethical manner. Healthcare organizations must ensure that patients and clinicians have access to information about how the AI system is making decisions and what factors are being considered.

Regularly Evaluate AI Systems for Bias: Healthcare organizations must regularly evaluate AI systems for bias and take steps to address any biases that are identified. This can involve developing policies and procedures for identifying and mitigating bias, as well as incorporating diverse data inputs to ensure that the system is not biased toward any particular patient population.

As the use of AI in healthcare continues to grow, legal and ethical considerations related to security are becoming increasingly important. Healthcare organizations must ensure that AI systems are used in a responsible and ethical manner, while also complying with legal and regulatory requirements related to security and privacy. This requires transparency, accountability, and fairness in AI systems, as well as regular risk assessments and evaluation for bias. By following best practices and staying up-to-date on the latest developments in legal and ethical requirements related to security in AI healthcare, healthcare organizations can ensure that they are using AI systems to improve patient outcomes while also protecting patient privacy and autonomy. It is essential that healthcare organizations prioritize security and privacy considerations from the start of the development and implementation of AI systems to ensure that they are used in a responsible and ethical manner. This requires collaboration among healthcare professionals, data scientists, and legal and regulatory experts to ensure that AI systems are developed and used in a way that benefits patients and society as a whole.

Addressing Security Challenges And Ensuring Compliance

As healthcare organizations continue to integrate AI systems into their operations, addressing security challenges and ensuring compliance with regulations is crucial. Cybersecurity threats, data breaches, and non-compliance with regulations can have severe consequences for patients, healthcare providers, and the organization as a whole. In this section, we will explore the key security challenges facing healthcare organizations and discuss strategies for ensuring compliance with regulations.

Addressing Security Challenges

Healthcare organizations face a range of security challenges related to AI systems, including data breaches, cyberattacks, and unauthorized access to patient information. These threats can result in significant harm to patients, including identity theft, financial losses, and compromised medical care. In addition, healthcare organizations may face reputational damage and legal liabilities in the event of a security breach.

To address these challenges, healthcare organizations should implement a range of security measures, including:

Risk Assessments: Healthcare organizations should conduct regular risk assessments to identify potential vulnerabilities in their systems and processes. This can include identifying potential threats and analyzing the likelihood and potential impact of these threats. Risk assessments can help organizations prioritize security measures and ensure that they are allocating resources effectively.

Access Controls: Healthcare organizations should implement access controls to ensure that only authorized personnel can access patient information. This can include multi-factor authentication, role-based access controls, and user activity monitoring. By limiting access to patient information, healthcare organizations can reduce the risk of unauthorized access and data breaches.

Data Encryption: Healthcare organizations should encrypt patient data to protect it from unauthorized access. Encryption can help to protect patient data in transit and at rest, reducing the risk of data breaches and unauthorized access. Healthcare organizations should also ensure that encryption keys are stored securely and are only accessible to authorized personnel.

Disaster Recovery: Healthcare organizations should have a disaster recovery plan in place to ensure that critical systems and data can be recovered in the event of a security breach or other disaster. This can include regular data backups, redundant systems, and a plan for restoring critical systems in the event of an outage.

Employee Training: Healthcare organizations should provide regular training to employees on cybersecurity best practices, including identifying phishing emails, protecting passwords, and reporting suspicious activity. By educating employees on security risks and best practices, healthcare organizations can reduce the risk of human error and improve overall security.

Ensuring Compliance

In addition to addressing security challenges, healthcare organizations must also ensure compliance with a range of regulations related to patient privacy and data protection. These regulations include the Health Insurance Portability and Accountability Act (HIPAA) in the United States, the General Data Protection Regulation (GDPR) in the European Union, and other regional and national regulations around the world.

To ensure compliance with these regulations, healthcare organizations should implement the following measures:

Data Governance: Healthcare organizations should establish clear policies and procedures for data governance, including data collection, storage, and sharing. This can include establishing data retention policies, ensuring that patient data is only shared with authorized parties, and implementing mechanisms for obtaining patient consent for data sharing.

Risk Assessments: Healthcare organizations should conduct regular risk assessments to identify potential vulnerabilities in their systems and processes related to data privacy and protection. This can include identifying potential threats to patient data and analyzing the likelihood and potential impact of these threats.

Data Security: Healthcare organizations should implement appropriate data security measures to protect patient data from unauthorized access, including data encryption, access controls, and user activity monitoring.

Data Breach Response: Healthcare organizations should have a plan in place for responding to data breaches, including notifying affected patients, regulatory authorities, and other relevant parties in a timely and transparent manner.

Compliance Audits: Healthcare organizations should conduct regular audits to ensure compliance with relevant regulations and identify areas for improvement. This can include conducting internal audits, as well as engaging external auditors to provide necessary technical expertise and an objective view of the organization's cybersecurity posture. Regular audits can help healthcare organizations stay on top of emerging threats and ensure that they are following best practices to protect patient data.

Incident Response Planning: Healthcare organizations should develop and implement an incident response plan to ensure that they are prepared to respond effectively to any security incidents that occur. This should include procedures for detecting and responding to security incidents, as well as protocols for communication and collaboration with relevant stakeholders, including patients, regulators, and law enforcement.

Education and Training: Healthcare organizations should provide regular education and training to employees on the importance of cybersecurity, as well as on the organization's policies and procedures for protecting patient data. This can include training on how to identify and respond to phishing attacks, how to create secure passwords, and how to handle sensitive patient information.

Risk Management: Healthcare organizations should conduct regular risk assessments to identify potential vulnerabilities and risks to patient data. This can include conducting penetration testing and vulnerability scanning to identify potential weaknesses in the organization's systems and applications. Once risks are identified, healthcare organizations should prioritize them and develop a plan to mitigate them.

Third-Party Management: Healthcare organizations should ensure that third-party vendors and partners that have access to patient data are also following best practices for cybersecurity. This can include conducting due diligence before partnering with a third party, as well as implementing security controls and regular audits to ensure compliance.

The use of AI in healthcare has the potential to transform patient care, improve outcomes, and reduce costs. However, as with any technology, there are risks associated with its use, particularly with regard to cybersecurity and data privacy. Healthcare organizations must take steps to ensure that they are protecting patient data and complying with relevant regulations. This includes implementing a comprehensive cybersecurity program, conducting regular risk assessments and compliance audits, and providing education and training to employees. By taking these steps, healthcare organizations can reap the benefits of AI while minimizing the risks.

Best Practices for Security and Privacy in AI Healthcare

As the use of AI in healthcare continues to grow, it is important for healthcare organizations to implement best practices for security and privacy to protect patient data and ensure compliance with relevant regulations. Here are some key best practices for security and privacy in AI healthcare:

Conduct regular risk assessments: Healthcare organizations should conduct regular risk assessments to identify potential vulnerabilities and risks to patient data. This can include conducting penetration testing and vulnerability scanning to identify potential weaknesses in the organization's systems and applications. Once risks are identified, healthcare organizations should prioritize them and develop a plan to mitigate them.

Implement a comprehensive cybersecurity program: A cybersecurity program is a set of policies, procedures, and practices designed to protect an organization's information assets, including patient data, from unauthorized access, theft, or destruction. A well-designed cybersecurity program will address the various aspects of cybersecurity, including access controls, network security, and incident response planning.

Use encryption and other security controls: Healthcare organizations should use encryption and other security controls to protect patient data. Encryption is the process of encoding data so that it can only be read by authorized users. Healthcare organizations should also implement access controls, such as firewalls and intrusion detection systems, to prevent unauthorized access to patient data.

Implement a data retention and destruction policy: Healthcare organizations should implement a data retention and destruction policy to ensure that patient data is only retained for as long as necessary and is properly destroyed when no longer needed. This can help minimize the risk of data breaches and other security incidents.

Train employees on cybersecurity best practices: Healthcare organizations should provide regular education and training to employees on the importance of cybersecurity, as well as on the organization's policies and procedures for protecting patient data. This can include training on how to identify and respond to phishing attacks, how to create secure passwords, and how to handle sensitive patient information.

Ensure third-party vendors and partners are following best practices: Healthcare organizations should ensure that third-party vendors and partners that have access to patient data are also following best practices for cybersecurity. This can include conducting due diligence before partnering with a third party, as well as implementing security controls and regular audits to ensure compliance.

Implement data privacy and protection policies: Healthcare organizations should implement policies and procedures for protecting patient privacy and complying with relevant regulations, such as HIPAA. This can include implementing strict access controls, limiting the use and disclosure of patient data, and providing patients with clear information about how their data is being used and protected.

Conduct regular compliance audits: Healthcare organizations should conduct regular compliance audits to ensure that they are following relevant regulations and industry standards for cybersecurity and data privacy. This can include conducting internal audits, as well as engaging external auditors to provide necessary technical expertise and an objective view of the organization's cybersecurity posture.

Develop and implement an incident response plan: Healthcare organizations should develop and implement an incident response plan to ensure that they are prepared to respond effectively to any security incidents that occur. This should include procedures for detecting and responding to security incidents, as well as protocols for communication and collaboration with relevant stakeholders, including patients, regulators, and law enforcement.

Continuously monitor and improve security and privacy practices: Healthcare organizations should continuously monitor and improve their security and privacy practices to stay on top of emerging threats and ensure that they are following best practices to protect patient data.

In conclusion, the use of AI in healthcare has the potential to transform patient care, improve outcomes, and reduce costs. However, healthcare organizations must take steps to ensure that they are protecting patient data and complying with relevant regulations. By implementing best practices for security and privacy, healthcare organizations can reap the benefits of AI while minimizing the risks.

CHAPTER 7:
CHALLENGES AND
LIMITATIONS OF AI
IN HEALTHCARE

While Artificial Intelligence (AI) has the potential to revolutionize healthcare, it is not without its challenges and limitations. Chapter 7 of this book addresses these issues and explores ways to mitigate them. The chapters in this section focus on the challenges of data quality and integration, privacy and security concerns, bias and fairness in AI algorithms, regulations and standards, and human factors and ethical considerations. These sections provide valuable insights into the potential pitfalls and limitations of using AI in healthcare, as well as the steps that can be taken to address them. By understanding and addressing these challenges, healthcare providers can optimize the use of AI to improve patient outcomes while minimizing the risks.

Data Quality And Integration

The success of AI in healthcare is heavily reliant on the quality and integration of data. With the exponential growth of healthcare data, it is crucial to ensure that data quality is not compromised, as this can have significant consequences on patient outcomes. Furthermore, integrating different data sources, such as electronic health records (EHRs), medical imaging, genomics, and real-time monitoring devices, is vital to enabling AI to deliver more accurate diagnoses, better personalized treatment plans, and improved patient outcomes.

In this section we will discuss the challenges associated with data quality and integration in AI healthcare and explore strategies to address them.

Data Quality in AI Healthcare

Data quality is a significant challenge in AI healthcare. It is essential to ensure that the data being used to train and test AI models is accurate, complete, and reliable. Poor-quality data can lead to biased models, inaccurate predictions, and potentially harmful treatment decisions.

One common issue is missing data, which can occur for various reasons, such as incomplete data entry, system errors, or patient refusal to disclose information. Missing data can cause issues with model training and testing and affect the overall quality of the model.

Another challenge is the accuracy of the data. Inaccurate data can occur due to data entry errors, incorrect coding, or outdated information. For example, if a patient's EHR contains incorrect information about their medical history or medications, this can lead to incorrect diagnoses and treatments.

To address these challenges, healthcare organizations should establish data quality assurance processes. These processes should include regular data audits, data cleaning and normalization, and verification of data accuracy and completeness.

Data Integration in AI Healthcare

Data integration is also a significant challenge in AI healthcare. Integrating data from different sources, such as EHRs, medical imaging, genomics, and real-time monitoring devices, is essential to creating more accurate and comprehensive patient profiles.

However, integrating data from different sources can be complicated. Each data source may have different data structures, data formats, and data definitions, making it challenging to integrate them seamlessly. Furthermore, integrating data from different sources can result in data duplication and data inconsistencies, further impacting data quality.

To address these challenges, healthcare organizations should establish data integration strategies that ensure seamless integration of data from various sources. These strategies should include standardizing data formats and definitions, ensuring data compatibility, and using data integration tools to automate the integration process.

AI models can also be used to integrate data from different sources. For example, natural language processing (NLP) can be used to extract relevant data from unstructured data sources, such as physician notes or medical literature.

Data quality and integration are critical challenges in AI healthcare. Ensuring that data is accurate, complete, and reliable is essential to creating unbiased and accurate AI models. Integrating data from different sources is crucial to creating more accurate and comprehensive patient profiles. By establishing data quality assurance processes and data integration strategies, healthcare organizations can improve the quality and integration of data, enabling AI to deliver better patient outcomes.

Privacy And Security

Privacy and security are critical aspects of healthcare that must be addressed when implementing AI technologies. As the use of AI in healthcare continues to grow, healthcare organizations must ensure that patient data is protected and secure. This section will explore the challenges and strategies for ensuring privacy and security in the context of AI in healthcare.

Challenges

There are several challenges that healthcare organizations face when it comes to ensuring privacy and security in the use of AI technologies. These include:

Data protection: The use of AI requires large amounts of patient data to be collected and analyzed. This data must be protected from unauthorized access and use.

Cybersecurity risks: As with any digital technology, AI is vulnerable to cyber-attacks that can compromise the security and privacy of patient data.

Regulatory compliance: Healthcare organizations must comply with various regulatory requirements related to privacy and security, such as HIPAA (Health Insurance Portability and Accountability Act) and GDPR (General Data Protection Regulation).

Lack of transparency: AI algorithms can be opaque and difficult to interpret, which can make it difficult to identify and address privacy and security issues.

Strategies

To address these challenges, healthcare organizations can implement several strategies for ensuring privacy and security in the use of AI technologies:

Data governance: Healthcare organizations should establish clear policies and procedures for the collection, storage, and use of patient data. This can include limiting access to sensitive data and implementing secure data sharing agreements with other organizations.

Encryption and access control: Healthcare organizations should implement encryption and access control measures to ensure that patient data is protected from unauthorized access.

Cybersecurity measures: Healthcare organizations should implement robust cybersecurity measures to protect against cyber-attacks. This can include implementing firewalls, intrusion detection and prevention systems, and regular vulnerability assessments.

Compliance monitoring: Healthcare organizations should regularly monitor their compliance with regulatory requirements related to privacy and security. This can include conducting regular audits and assessments of their security posture.

Transparency and explainability: Healthcare organizations should strive to make AI algorithms more transparent and explainable. This can include implementing tools for algorithmic accountability and providing clear explanations of how AI algorithms are used and how they make decisions.

Privacy and security are critical aspects of healthcare that must be addressed when implementing AI technologies. Healthcare organizations must take proactive steps to protect patient data and ensure compliance with relevant regulations. By implementing robust data governance, encryption and access control measures, cybersecurity measures, compliance monitoring, and transparency and explainability strategies, healthcare organizations can mitigate the risks associated with the use of AI in healthcare and ensure that patient data is protected and secure.

Bias And Fairness

Artificial Intelligence (AI) has the potential to transform healthcare by improving patient outcomes and reducing costs. However, one of the major challenges in AI healthcare is the presence of bias and fairness issues. Bias refers to the systematic errors in the data or algorithms that lead to inaccurate or unfair outcomes. Fairness refers to the equitable treatment of individuals regardless of their characteristics such as race, gender, or age. In this section, we will explore the various types of bias and fairness issues in AI healthcare and their impact on patient care.

Types of Bias in AI Healthcare

There are several types of bias in AI healthcare, including:

Data bias: Data bias occurs when the data used to train an AI algorithm is not representative of the entire population or is biased in some way. For example, if a dataset used to train a predictive model for cancer diagnosis only includes data from one ethnicity, the algorithm may not be able to accurately predict cancer in patients from other ethnicities.

Algorithmic bias: Algorithmic bias occurs when the algorithm itself is biased, resulting in unfair outcomes. For example, an algorithm designed to predict hospital readmissions may be biased against patients from low-income neighborhoods, resulting in them being unfairly flagged for readmission.

User bias: User bias occurs when the individuals who use the AI system introduce their own biases into the system. For example, a doctor who uses an AI system to diagnose patients may be biased against certain patient populations, resulting in inaccurate diagnoses.

Impact of Bias on Patient Care

Bias in AI healthcare can have a significant impact on patient care. For example, if an algorithm is biased against a certain population, patients from that population may not receive the appropriate care. This can lead to missed diagnoses, delayed treatments, and poor outcomes. Additionally, bias can undermine trust in the healthcare system, leading to patient dissatisfaction and decreased use of healthcare services.

Types of Fairness in AI Healthcare

There are several types of fairness in AI healthcare, including:

Procedural fairness: Procedural fairness refers to the fairness of the process used to make decisions. For example, if an algorithm is used to determine which patients receive certain treatments, the process used to make those decisions should be transparent and unbiased.

Distributive fairness: Distributive fairness refers to the fairness of the outcomes of the decisions. For example, if an algorithm is used to allocate healthcare resources, the distribution of those resources should be fair and equitable.

Representational fairness: Representational fairness refers to the fairness of the data used to train the algorithm. The data should be representative of the entire population and not biased in any way.

Addressing Bias and Fairness in AI Healthcare

There are several ways to address bias and fairness in AI healthcare:

Improve data quality: To address data bias, it is important to ensure that the data used to train AI algorithms is representative of the entire population and not biased in any way. This can be achieved by collecting data from diverse sources and ensuring that the data is cleaned and pre-processed before it is used.

Use bias detection tools: To address algorithmic bias, it is important to use bias detection tools to identify and eliminate any biases in the algorithm. These tools can be used to monitor the algorithm's output and identify any patterns of bias.

Incorporate diversity and inclusion: To address user bias, it is important to incorporate diversity and inclusion into the AI system design. This can be achieved by including diverse perspectives in the design and development process and providing training to users to ensure that they are aware of their biases.

Evaluate fairness: To address fairness, it is important to evaluate the fairness of the AI system using metrics such as accuracy, precision, and recall. These metrics can be used to evaluate the effectiveness and fairness of AI models in healthcare. In addition to these metrics, there are also several best practices that can be followed to promote fairness and reduce bias in AI healthcare:

Ensure diverse representation in training data: One of the main ways to reduce bias in AI healthcare is to ensure that the training data used to develop models is diverse and representative of the patient population. This can involve collecting data from a variety of sources and ensuring that the data is balanced across different demographics.

Use explainable algorithms: To ensure that AI healthcare models are transparent and accountable, it is important to use algorithms that can be easily explained and understood. This can help to identify potential biases and make sure that models are fair and accurate.

Regularly evaluate models for bias: AI healthcare models should be regularly evaluated for potential biases and tested to ensure that they are fair and accurate. This can involve running tests on new data sets or monitoring models in real-time to detect any biases that may arise. Involve diverse stakeholders in development: To ensure that AI healthcare models are inclusive and equitable, it is important to involve a diverse group of stakeholders in the development process. This can include patients, healthcare providers, and other experts who can provide different perspectives on the needs and concerns of different patient groups.

Address bias when it is identified: If biases are identified in AI healthcare models, it is important to take steps to address them. This may involve adjusting the training data or algorithm used or implementing other strategies to reduce bias and promote fairness.

In summary, addressing bias and promoting fairness in AI healthcare is essential for ensuring that these technologies are effective, accurate, and accessible to all patients. This requires a thoughtful approach to data collection and model development, ongoing monitoring and evaluation, and involving diverse stakeholders in the process. By following best practices and prioritizing fairness and inclusivity in the development of AI healthcare applications, we can create technologies that benefit all patients and improve healthcare outcomes for everyone.

Regulations and Standards

The use of AI in healthcare is subject to a wide range of regulations and standards that are designed to ensure patient safety, privacy, and data security. These regulations can vary depending on the country or region where the healthcare organization operates, as well as the specific type of AI technology being used. Some of the most important regulations and standards that healthcare organizations should be aware of when implementing AI include:

General Data Protection Regulation (GDPR): The GDPR is a set of regulations established by the European Union to protect the privacy of personal data. It applies to all companies that process personal data of individuals residing in the EU, including healthcare organizations. The regulation sets out specific requirements for the collection, storage, processing, and sharing of personal data, as well as guidelines for obtaining informed consent from patients.

Health Insurance Portability and Accountability Act (HIPAA): HIPAA is a set of regulations established in the United States to protect the privacy and security of patient health information. It applies to all healthcare organizations that collect, store, process, or transmit patient health information, including those using AI technology. The regulation sets out specific requirements for the protection of patient health information, including guidelines for data storage and transmission, data access controls, and breach notification procedures.

Medical Device Regulation (MDR): The MDR is a set of regulations established by the European Union to ensure the safety and effectiveness of medical devices, including those that use AI technology. The regulation sets out specific requirements for the design, manufacture, and testing of medical devices, as well as guidelines for post-market surveillance and reporting of adverse events.

Food and Drug Administration (FDA) regulations: In the United States, the FDA is responsible for regulating medical devices and software, including those that use AI technology. The agency has established specific guidelines for the development, testing, and approval of medical devices and software, as well as guidelines for post-market surveillance and reporting of adverse events.

Ethical guidelines: Healthcare organizations should also consider the ethical implications of using AI in healthcare. The use of AI can raise several ethical concerns, including issues of bias, fairness, and transparency. Organizations should consider the potential impact of AI on patient privacy and autonomy, as well as the potential risks associated with the use of AI in decision-making processes.

Standards for interoperability: AI systems in healthcare rely on the exchange of data across different systems and platforms. Standards for interoperability are essential for ensuring that different AI systems can communicate and exchange data in a standardized and secure manner. Organizations should consider the use of established standards, such as Fast Healthcare Interoperability Resources (FHIR), to ensure that their AI systems are interoperable with other systems and platforms.

To ensure compliance with these regulations and standards, healthcare organizations should establish clear policies and procedures for the use of AI technology. These policies should address issues such as data security, privacy, and informed consent, as well as guidelines for the development, testing, and deployment of AI systems. Organizations should also conduct regular audits to ensure compliance with relevant regulations and identify areas for improvement. Engaging with regulatory bodies and seeking guidance from legal and ethical experts can also help organizations navigate the complex regulatory landscape surrounding the use of AI in healthcare.

Human Factors And Ethical Considerations

As artificial intelligence (AI) continues to become a critical component in healthcare, it is essential to consider human factors and ethical considerations to ensure that the technology is used effectively and safely. While AI has the potential to improve patient outcomes, reduce costs, and increase efficiency, it can also lead to unintended consequences and ethical dilemmas if not implemented with care. This section will discuss the importance of human factors and ethical considerations in AI healthcare, the challenges that may arise, and best practices for addressing them.

Human Factors in AI Healthcare

Human factors refer to the physical, cognitive, and organizational aspects of a system that affect the performance and well-being of the people using it. In the context of AI healthcare, human factors involve the interaction between healthcare providers, patients, and AI systems. The design of AI systems should take into account the human factors that can influence their effectiveness and adoption.

One critical human factor in AI healthcare is usability. AI systems should be designed to be easy to use, intuitive, and minimize the cognitive load on healthcare providers. Poorly designed systems can lead to errors, inefficiencies, and frustration among healthcare providers, leading to low adoption rates and compromised patient care. To ensure usability, designers should involve end-users in the design process and conduct user testing to identify and address usability issues.

Another important factor is the communication between healthcare providers and AI systems. Healthcare providers should have a clear understanding of the AI system's capabilities and limitations to make informed decisions about patient care. On the other hand, AI systems should provide clear and concise information to healthcare providers to avoid confusion or misinterpretation of data. Effective communication can improve the accuracy and efficiency of AI systems while minimizing the risk of errors.

Finally, human factors also include organizational factors such as culture and workflow. AI systems should be integrated into the healthcare organization's culture and workflow to ensure their effective adoption and use. The organization should have policies and procedures in place for the responsible use of AI systems, including training, monitoring, and accountability.

CHAPTER 8: FUTURE OF AI IN HEALTHCARE

rtificial Intelligence (AI) is rapidly advancing and changing the landscape of healthcare. Chapter 8 of this book explores the emerging trends and potential future applications of AI in healthcare. The sections in this chapter focus on the intersection of AI with robotics, neuroscience, genomics, and healthcare access, and highlight the opportunities and challenges associated with these applications. By understanding the potential of AI in these areas, healthcare providers can prepare for and take advantage of the future of AI in healthcare.

Emerging Trends

Artificial intelligence (AI) has the potential to transform the healthcare industry by enabling more personalized care, improving the accuracy of diagnoses, and streamlining clinical workflows. However, as the field of AI continues to evolve, new trends are emerging that have the potential to further transform healthcare in the coming years. This section explores some of the most promising emerging trends in AI healthcare.

Use of AI for Diagnosis and Treatment

One of the most promising applications of AI in healthcare is its ability to improve the accuracy of diagnoses and treatments. With the help of machine learning algorithms, AI systems can analyze vast amounts of patient data to identify patterns and make predictions about a patient's condition. This can help clinicians make more accurate diagnoses, choose the most effective treatments, and monitor patients more closely.

For example, researchers are developing AI algorithms that can analyze medical images to identify signs of disease, such as cancerous tumors. In one study, researchers at Stanford University developed an AI system that can accurately diagnose skin cancer using images of moles and other skin lesions. The system was able to achieve a level of accuracy that was comparable to that of experienced dermatologists.

Similarly, AI systems are being developed to help clinicians identify patterns in patient data that could indicate the early stages of a disease. For example, an AI algorithm developed by researchers at Harvard University and Brigham and Women's Hospital can analyze electronic health records to identify patients who are at risk of developing sepsis, a life-threatening condition that can be difficult to diagnose.

Use of AI for Personalized Medicine

Another emerging trend in AI healthcare is the use of AI to develop personalized treatment plans for patients. By analyzing patient data, including genetic information, medical history, and lifestyle factors, AI systems can help clinicians develop customized treatment plans that are tailored to each patient's unique needs.

For example, researchers at the University of Pennsylvania are using AI to develop personalized treatment plans for patients with cancer. By analyzing the genetic mutations present in a patient's tumor, the AI system can identify which drugs are likely to be most effective in treating the cancer.

Similarly, researchers are developing AI algorithms that can analyze data from wearable devices, such as fitness trackers, to monitor a patient's health in real-time. This data can be used to identify patterns that could indicate the early stages of a disease or to track the effectiveness of a treatment plan.

Use of AI for Drug Discovery

AI is also being used to accelerate the drug discovery process. Traditionally, drug discovery has been a time-consuming and expensive process, but AI has the potential to streamline this process by identifying potential drug candidates more quickly and accurately.

For example, researchers at Insilico Medicine are using AI to develop new drugs to treat a range of diseases, including cancer and Alzheimer's disease. By analyzing vast amounts of data on the molecular structure of drugs and their interactions with cells in the body, the AI system can identify potential drug candidates that are more likely to be effective.

Similarly, researchers at BenevolentAI are using AI to identify potential drug candidates for diseases such as Parkinson's disease and motor neuron disease. By analyzing vast amounts of data from scientific journals, clinical trials, and other sources, the AI system can identify potential drug candidates that have not yet been explored by human researchers.

Predictive Analytics

Predictive analytics is a type of AI that uses statistical algorithms and machine learning techniques to analyze historical and current data to predict future outcomes. In healthcare, predictive analytics can be used to identify patients at high risk of developing a particular condition or disease.

For example, predictive analytics can be used to identify patients at high risk of developing diabetes based on their medical history, lifestyle factors, and genetics. Healthcare providers can then use this information to intervene early and prevent the onset of the disease.

Precision Medicine

Precision medicine is a personalized approach to healthcare that takes into account an individual's genetics, environment, and lifestyle to develop tailored treatment plans. AI is playing a critical role in advancing precision medicine by enabling healthcare providers to analyze large datasets and identify patterns and insights that would be impossible to detect manually.

For example, AI can be used to analyze genomic data to identify specific gene mutations that are associated with certain diseases. This information can then be used to develop targeted treatments that are more effective and have fewer side effects.

Medical Imaging

Medical imaging is an area of healthcare that is particularly well-suited to the use of AI. AI algorithms can analyze medical images, such as X-rays and MRI scans, to identify patterns and anomalies that are difficult for human radiologists to detect.
For example, AI can be used to analyze medical images to identify early signs of cancer or other diseases. This can lead to earlier detection and more effective treatment.

Virtual Assistants and Chatbots

Virtual assistants and chatbots have already started to revolutionize healthcare. These AI-driven tools can identify patients at high risk of readmission, engage patients in real-time conversations, and deliver personalized care, reminders, and medication instructions.

For example, Buoy Health's AI-powered chatbot helps patients understand their symptoms and provides them with relevant health information. Similarly, Your.MD's chatbot allows patients to enter their symptoms and receive personalized health recommendations.

Wearables and IoT Devices

Wearables and Internet of Things (IoT) devices have been growing in popularity for years. The healthcare industry has taken note of the trend and is beginning to adopt these technologies to enhance patient care. Wearables and IoT devices can collect data and provide insights that help healthcare providers diagnose and treat patients more effectively.

For instance, Fitbit has already partnered with a number of healthcare providers to integrate its wearables with electronic health records (EHRs) and provide real-time health data to healthcare providers. Similarly, Philips has developed an IoT-enabled wearable biosensor that can continuously monitor patients' vital signs and provide early warnings for potential health issues.

Edge AI

Edge AI is an emerging trend that involves running AI algorithms on edge devices, such as smartphones and wearables, rather than in the cloud. By running AI algorithms on edge devices, healthcare providers can reduce latency and improve response times, making it possible to deliver real-time care and diagnostics.

For instance, Edge AI can be used in remote patient monitoring to analyze patient data in real-time and provide feedback to healthcare providers. It can also be used in emergency response situations to quickly analyze medical images and provide real-time diagnosis and treatment recommendations.

Artificial Intelligence And Robotics

Artificial intelligence (AI) and robotics are two of the most transformative technologies in healthcare today. While each technology has its own unique capabilities and applications, when combined, they have the potential to revolutionize the way healthcare is delivered. In this chapter, we will explore the emerging trends and applications of AI and robotics in healthcare.

The Rise of Robotics in Healthcare Robotics has been used in healthcare for decades, primarily in surgical procedures, but recent advances in technology have enabled the development of more sophisticated robots that can perform a wider range of tasks. For example, robots are now being used to assist with physical therapy, monitor patients, and even dispense medication.

One of the most exciting applications of robotics in healthcare is in the area of surgical robotics. Robotic surgical systems enable surgeons to perform procedures with greater precision and control, leading to better patient outcomes and shorter recovery times. In addition, robotic surgical systems are less invasive than traditional surgery, resulting in reduced pain and scarring for patients.

The Role of AI in Robotics AI is a critical component of robotics in healthcare. By analyzing vast amounts of data, AI algorithms can help robots make more accurate decisions and improve their performance over time. For example, AI can be used to help robots navigate complex environments, such as hospital corridors or patient rooms, and to identify and avoid obstacles.

AI can also be used to enhance the capabilities of robots in healthcare. For example, AI algorithms can be used to analyze medical images and help robots identify and locate tumors or other abnormalities with greater accuracy.

Applications of AI and Robotics in Healthcare

The combination of AI and robotics has led to a wide range of innovative applications in healthcare. Here are some examples:

Robotic surgery: As mentioned earlier, robotic surgical systems enable surgeons to perform procedures with greater precision and control, leading to better patient outcomes and shorter recovery times.

Physical therapy: Robots can be used to assist patients with physical therapy, providing personalized exercises and monitoring progress.

Elderly care: Robots can be used to assist elderly patients with daily activities, such as getting dressed or preparing meals.

Medication management: Robots can be used to dispense medication and ensure that patients receive the correct dose at the correct time.

Monitoring: Robots can be used to monitor patients in hospital settings, providing real-time data on vital signs and alerting healthcare providers to potential issues.

Challenges and Limitations

While the potential benefits of AI and robotics in healthcare are significant, there are also several challenges and limitations that must be addressed. One of the biggest challenges is the cost of implementing these technologies, as they can be expensive to develop and deploy.

Another challenge is the potential for job displacement. As robots become more sophisticated, there is a risk that they may replace human workers in certain tasks, leading to job losses.

Finally, there are also ethical considerations to be taken into account. For example, there may be concerns around patient privacy and data security when using robots and AI in healthcare settings.

Future Directions

Despite these challenges, the future of AI and robotics in healthcare looks bright. With ongoing advancements in technology, it is likely that we will see even more innovative applications of these technologies in the years to come

One area of particular interest is the development of collaborative robots, or cobots, which are designed to work alongside human healthcare providers to enhance their capabilities and improve patient outcomes.

In addition, there is a growing focus on developing robots and AI systems that are more adaptable and flexible, enabling them to perform a wider range of tasks and operate in a variety of healthcare settings.

As the healthcare industry continues to evolve, it is clear that AI and robotics will play an increasingly important role in delivering high-quality, personalized care to patients.

Artificial Intelligence And Neuroscience

Neuroscience is the study of the nervous system, including the brain, spinal cord, and network of nerves throughout the body. It seeks to understand how the nervous system functions and how it gives rise to behavior, cognition, and consciousness. AI, on the other hand, is a technology that has revolutionized the way we process information, enabling machines to learn, reason, and make decisions without human intervention.

The integration of AI and neuroscience has the potential to unlock a new level of understanding of the brain and its functions. AI tools can help analyze the vast amounts of data generated by neuroscientific research, leading to new insights into how the brain works and how it can be treated when damaged or diseased. In this chapter, we explore the current state and future possibilities of AI and neuroscience.

Neuroimaging

Neuroimaging is a technique used in neuroscience to produce images of the brain's structure and function. It is used to study the brain's activity during different tasks and to identify abnormalities that may be associated with neurological disorders such as Alzheimer's disease, Parkinson's disease, and schizophrenia. However, the analysis of neuroimaging data can be time-consuming and challenging due to the complexity of the data.

AI can help streamline the analysis of neuroimaging data, making it easier and faster to identify patterns and anomalies. For example, machine learning algorithms can be trained to recognize specific features in neuroimaging data that are associated with certain disorders. This can lead to more accurate diagnoses and more effective treatments.

Brain-Computer Interfaces

Brain-Computer Interfaces (BCIs) are devices that enable direct communication between the brain and a computer or other electronic device. They work by translating signals from the brain into commands that can be used to control a computer or other device. BCIs have the potential to transform the lives of people with disabilities, allowing them to control prosthetic limbs or other devices using their thoughts.

AI can help improve the accuracy and efficiency of BCIs by enhancing their ability to interpret signals from the brain. Machine learning algorithms can be used to analyze patterns in the brain signals and identify the intended actions more accurately. This can lead to more precise control of prosthetic limbs or other devices and improve the quality of life for people with disabilities.

Neuroprosthetics

Neuroprosthetics are devices that replace or enhance the function of the nervous system. They can be used to restore lost sensory or motor function or to treat neurological disorders. Examples of neuroprosthetics include cochlear implants, deep brain stimulators, and spinal cord stimulators.

AI can help improve the design and functionality of neuroprosthetics. For example, machine learning algorithms can be used to analyze the signals from implanted devices and adjust the stimulation settings to optimize their effectiveness. This can lead to better outcomes for patients and reduce the need for manual adjustments by healthcare providers.

Neuropharmacology

Neuropharmacology is the study of how drugs affect the nervous system. It is used to develop new treatments for neurological and psychiatric disorders. However, the process of drug discovery and development can be time-consuming and costly.

AI can help accelerate the drug discovery process by predicting the effectiveness of potential drugs before they are tested in humans. Machine learning algorithms can be trained to analyze large datasets of chemical compounds and predict which ones are most likely to be effective. This can lead to more efficient drug discovery and potentially faster development of new treatments for neurological disorders.

Ethical Considerations

The integration of AI and neuroscience raises a number of ethical considerations. For example, BCIs raise concerns about privacy and security, as the devices require access to the brain's signals, which are highly personal and sensitive. There are also concerns about the potential misuse of neuroimaging data, as it could be used to infer account. There are also concerns about the potential misuse of neuroimaging data, as it could be used to infer sensitive information about individuals, such as their political views, sexual orientation, or mental health status. It is important for researchers to ensure that the privacy and confidentiality of individuals' data is protected.

Another challenge in the application of AI in neuroscience is the lack of interpretability of many machine learning models. While these models can accurately predict outcomes based on brain imaging data, it is often unclear how they arrived at their conclusions. This lack of transparency can make it difficult for clinicians and researchers to understand and trust the results of AI models.

In conclusion, AI has the potential to revolutionize the field of neuroscience by improving our understanding of the brain and developing new treatments for neurological disorders. However, there are still significant challenges to be addressed, including the ethical implications of brain-computer interfaces and the lack of interpretability of many AI models. By addressing these challenges, researchers and clinicians can work towards realizing the full potential of AI in neuroscience.

Artificial Intelligence And Genomics

Genomics is the study of an organism's genetic material, including its DNA sequence and the functional roles of its genes. Over the past decade, advances in DNA sequencing technologies have made it possible to sequence entire genomes at a relatively low cost. This has led to an explosion of genomic data, creating new opportunities for personalized medicine and drug development. At the same time, analyzing and interpreting this data is a major challenge, requiring sophisticated computational tools and techniques. AI has emerged as a powerful tool for analyzing and interpreting genomic data, with the potential to transform the field of genomics.

One of the primary applications of AI in genomics is the identification of genetic variations associated with disease. These variations can be single nucleotide polymorphisms (SNPs), insertions or deletions, or structural variations. Machine learning algorithms can be trained to analyze genomic data and identify these variations, as well as to predict the likelihood of developing a particular disease based on an individual's genetic makeup. This information can be used to develop personalized treatment plans and to identify individuals who are at high risk of developing certain diseases.

AI can also be used to develop new drugs and therapies based on an individual's genetic makeup. For example, AI can be used to identify genetic targets for drug development and to predict the efficacy of different drugs based on an individual's genomic data. This approach, known as pharmacogenomics, has the potential to revolutionize drug development by enabling the development of personalized drugs that are tailored to an individual's specific genetic makeup.

Another application of AI in genomics is the analysis of large-scale genomic data sets. The human genome consists of more than 3 billion base pairs, making it one of the largest data sets in existence. Analyzing this data requires sophisticated computational tools and techniques. Machine learning algorithms can be trained to analyze large-scale genomic data sets and identify patterns and relationships between genes, proteins, and diseases. This information can be used to develop new diagnostic tools and treatments for a wide range of diseases.

However, there are also significant challenges to the use of AI in genomics. One of the primary challenges is the need for large, high-quality data sets. AI algorithms require large amounts of data to be trained effectively, and the quality of the data is critical to the accuracy of the predictions made by the algorithms. In addition, there are concerns about the privacy and security of genomic data, as this information is highly sensitive and could be used for discriminatory purposes if it falls into the wrong hands.

Another challenge is the need for interpretability and transparency of AI models. The decisions made by machine learning algorithms can be difficult to interpret, making it challenging for clinicians and researchers to understand how the models arrived at their conclusions. This lack of transparency can also make it difficult to gain regulatory approval for AI-based diagnostic tools and treatments.

In conclusion, AI has the potential to transform the field of genomics by enabling personalized medicine and drug development and by providing new insights into the relationships between genes, proteins, and diseases. However, there are significant challenges to the use of AI in genomics, including the need for large, high-quality data sets, concerns about the privacy and security of genomic data, and the need for interpretability and transparency of AI models. By addressing these challenges, researchers and clinicians can work towards realizing the full potential of AI in genomics.

Artificial Intelligence And Healthcare Access

AI has the potential to revolutionize healthcare access by enhancing the quality of care, improving patient outcomes, and reducing healthcare costs. However, access to healthcare services and resources remains a significant challenge for millions of people worldwide. AI can help address this issue by providing innovative solutions that enable people to receive timely, affordable, and high-quality healthcare services.

One of the most significant benefits of AI in healthcare access is its ability to improve diagnostic accuracy and speed. AI-powered diagnostic tools can help healthcare professionals to accurately diagnose diseases and conditions quickly, reducing the need for unnecessary testing and procedures. This, in turn, can help to reduce healthcare costs, improve patient outcomes, and increase access to healthcare services for underserved populations.

AI can also be used to improve the efficiency and effectiveness of healthcare delivery systems. For example, AI-powered chatbots and virtual assistants can provide patients with real-time medical advice and support, reducing the need for in-person consultations and appointments. This can be particularly beneficial for people living in remote areas or those with limited mobility, who may find it challenging to access traditional healthcare services.

AI can also help to improve the delivery of healthcare services by automating administrative tasks and streamlining healthcare operations. This can help healthcare professionals to focus on providing high-quality patient care, while reducing administrative burdens and improving overall healthcare efficiency.

Another potential application of AI in healthcare access is the development of personalized treatment plans. AI algorithms can analyze large amounts of patient data to identify trends and patterns, which can be used to develop customized treatment plans that are tailored to individual patient needs. This can help to improve treatment outcomes, reduce healthcare costs, and enhance patient satisfaction.

However, there are also challenges and limitations to the use of AI in healthcare access. One significant concern is the potential for AI to exacerbate existing healthcare disparities, particularly for vulnerable and underserved populations. For example, AI-powered healthcare services may not be accessible to people who lack access to the internet or cannot afford the necessary technology. Additionally, there is a risk that AI algorithms may perpetuate biases and discrimination, particularly if they are trained on biased or limited data sets.

Another concern is the potential for AI to replace human healthcare professionals, particularly in low-resource settings where healthcare providers may already be in short supply. While AI has the potential to improve healthcare efficiency and reduce costs, it is essential to ensure that it is used to augment rather than replace human healthcare professionals, particularly in areas where human expertise is critical.

In conclusion, AI has the potential to improve healthcare access and reduce healthcare disparities by enhancing the quality of care, improving patient outcomes, and reducing healthcare costs. However, it is essential to address the challenges and limitations associated with the use of AI in healthcare access, particularly the potential for exacerbating existing disparities and replacing human healthcare professionals. By addressing these challenges, AI can be used to provide innovative solutions that enhance access to high-quality healthcare services for all.

CHAPTER 9:
CASE STUDIES
AND PRACTICAL
APPLICATIONS

T his section of this book focuses on the practical applications of AI in healthcare. Chapter 9 includes case studies of successful AI implementations in healthcare, an exploration of AI-based healthcare startups, and best practices for AI adoption in healthcare. These sections provide insights into how AI is being used to improve patient outcomes and the challenges and best practices associated with implementing these technologies.

Artificial intelligence (AI) is transforming healthcare in various ways, from drug discovery and personalized medicine to predictive analytics and medical imaging. In this chapter, we will explore some case studies that illustrate how AI is being used in healthcare to improve patient outcomes, reduce costs, and enhance the efficiency of healthcare delivery.

IBM Watson Health: Oncology and Genomics

IBM Watson Health is an AI-powered platform that aims to improve cancer care and genomics. The platform can analyze vast amounts of data from medical journals, clinical trials, and patient records to provide personalized treatment recommendations to clinicians.

One example of the use of IBM Watson Health is at the MD Anderson Cancer Center, where the platform has been used to analyze patient data and generate treatment plans for cancer patients. The platform uses natural language processing to read through patient records and medical literature, and then generates a list of potential treatment options based on the patient's specific cancer type and genomic profile.

According to a study published in the Journal of Clinical Oncology, patients who received treatment based on Watson's recommendations had an overall survival rate of 80%, compared to 67% for patients who received standard treatment. This case study highlights how AI can improve cancer care by providing clinicians with personalized treatment recommendations based on genomic and clinical data.

Viz.ai: Stroke Detection

Viz.ai is an AI-powered platform that uses deep learning algorithms to analyze medical images and detect signs of stroke. The platform can quickly analyze CT scans and MRI images to identify patients with signs of large vessel occlusion (LVO), a type of stroke that requires urgent treatment.

Once the platform identifies a patient with signs of LVO, it alerts the neurologist, allowing them to quickly evaluate the patient and initiate treatment. This can significantly reduce the time it takes to diagnose and treat stroke patients, leading to better outcomes and reduced healthcare costs.

According to a study published in the Journal of NeuroInterventional Surgery, Viz.ai reduced the time it took to diagnose and treat stroke patients by an average of 92 minutes. This case study illustrates how AI can improve stroke care by quickly identifying patients who require urgent treatment and alerting clinicians.

AliveCor: ECG Analysis

AliveCor is an AI-powered platform that uses machine learning algorithms to analyze electrocardiograms (ECGs) and detect signs of arrhythmia. The platform can quickly analyze ECGs taken with a smartphone or other mobile device and provide real-time feedback to patients and clinicians.

The platform can also provide personalized treatment recommendations based on the patient's ECG results and medical history. This can help clinicians identify patients who require further evaluation and treatment, leading to better outcomes and reduced healthcare costs.

According to a study published in the Journal of the American Medical Association, AliveCor's AI algorithms were able to accurately detect atrial fibrillation, the most common type of arrhythmia, with a sensitivity of 93% and a specificity of 84%. This case study highlights how AI can improve cardiac care by quickly and accurately identifying patients with arrhythmias.

AI in Radiology

In recent years, AI has been applied to radiology to improve the accuracy and speed of image interpretation, as well as reduce the workload of radiologists. One example is the use of AI in mammography for breast cancer screening. In a study published in Nature, researchers developed an AI model that could accurately detect breast cancer in mammography images with a sensitivity of 94.5% and a specificity of 89.8%, which is comparable to the performance of human radiologists. Another study found that an AI model could improve the accuracy of CT scan interpretation for the diagnosis of pulmonary nodules.

One company that has developed AI solutions for radiology is Aidoc, which uses deep learning algorithms to analyze medical images and provide insights to radiologists. Aidoc's solutions can detect and prioritize critical cases, such as cases of stroke or pulmonary embolism, which require urgent attention. The company's algorithms have been trained on millions of images and have been validated in clinical trials.

Another example of AI in radiology is the use of natural language processing (NLP) to extract information from radiology reports. NLP can be used to identify and extract specific information, such as the location and size of a tumor, from radiology reports, which can be used to improve the accuracy of cancer diagnosis and treatment planning. One company that offers NLP solutions for radiology is Radboudumc, which has developed an NLP algorithm that can extract relevant information from radiology reports with a high degree of accuracy.

Overall, AI has shown great promise in improving the accuracy and efficiency of radiology, as well as reducing the workload of radiologists. However, there are also challenges associated with the implementation of AI in radiology, such as the need for large and diverse datasets for training AI models, as well as the need to ensure that AI solutions are validated and tested in clinical settings before they are used in practice.

AI in Personalized Medicine

Personalized medicine is an emerging field that seeks to tailor medical treatment to the specific needs of individual patients based on their genetic and other relevant information. AI has the potential to revolutionize personalized medicine by enabling the analysis of large and complex datasets, such as genomic data, and identifying patterns and associations that can be used to develop personalized treatment plans.

One company that has developed AI solutions for personalized medicine is Tempus, which uses machine learning algorithms to analyze large datasets of genomic, clinical, and other relevant data to develop personalized treatment plans for cancer patients. The company's solutions have been used to develop personalized treatment plans for thousands of patients and have shown promising results in improving patient outcomes.

Another example of AI in personalized medicine is the use of AI algorithms to predict drug response based on genomic data. One study found that an AI model could accurately predict drug response in cancer patients based on their genomic data, which could be used to develop personalized treatment plans.

While AI has the potential to greatly improve personalized medicine, there are also challenges associated with the implementation of AI in this field. These include the need for large and diverse datasets for training AI models, as well as the need to ensure that AI solutions are validated and tested in clinical settings before they are used in practice.

Babylon Health

Babylon Health is a telemedicine company that uses AI to provide virtual consultations and diagnosis. The company's AI-powered chatbot, known as the Babylon Health Assistant, uses natural language processing to understand patients' symptoms and provide personalized health advice. The chatbot can also be used to book virtual appointments with healthcare providers, order prescriptions, and provide mental health support.

Babylon Health has been used by numerous healthcare providers in the UK and other parts of the world. For example, the company has partnered with the UK's National Health Service (NHS) to provide virtual consultations to patients. The partnership allows patients to access healthcare services remotely, reducing the need for in-person appointments and potentially reducing the risk of exposure to COVID-19.

In addition to these examples, there are many other ways in which AI is being used in healthcare. For example, AI is being used to develop predictive models for patient outcomes, analyze medical images, and automate administrative tasks such as scheduling and billing.

Overall, AI has the potential to revolutionize healthcare by improving the accuracy and efficiency of diagnosis and treatment decisions, reducing healthcare costs, and improving patient outcomes. However, there are also challenges and limitations associated with the use of AI in healthcare, including concerns around privacy and security, bias and fairness, and the need to ensure that AI is used ethically and responsibly. As AI continues to advance, it will be important for healthcare providers and regulators to work together to address these challenges and ensure that the benefits of AI are realized while minimizing its risks.

Artificial Intelligence-Based Healthcare Startups

As the demand for innovative healthcare solutions increases, so does the number of AI-based healthcare startups. These startups are leveraging AI technology to develop new tools, software, and platforms that can help healthcare providers deliver better care, improve patient outcomes, and reduce costs.

AI-based healthcare startups are disrupting the traditional

healthcare industry, providing solutions that are faster, more accurate, and less expensive than traditional approaches. Some of the most promising startups in the field of AI in healthcare include:

Paige.AI: Paige.AI is a New York-based startup that uses AI to help pathologists diagnose cancer. The company has developed a platform that can analyze large amounts of pathology data and provide pathologists with insights that can help them make more accurate diagnoses.

Zebra Medical Vision: Zebra Medical Vision is an Israeli startup that uses AI to analyze medical images. The company's software can detect a range of medical conditions, including fractures, tumors, and other abnormalities.

AiCure: AiCure is a New York-based startup that uses AI to monitor patient adherence to medication. The company's software uses facial recognition technology to confirm that patients are taking their medication as prescribed.

Prognos: Prognos is a New York-based startup that uses AI to predict disease outcomes. The company's platform can analyze large amounts of patient data and provide healthcare providers with insights into patient outcomes.

Enlitic: Enlitic is a San Francisco-based startup that uses AI to analyze medical images. The company's software can detect a range of medical conditions, including fractures, tumors, and other abnormalities.

PathAI: PathAI is a Boston-based startup that uses AI to help pathologists diagnose cancer. The company's platform can analyze large amounts of pathology data and provide pathologists with insights that can help them make more accurate diagnoses.

Lunit: Lunit is a Korean startup that uses AI to analyze medical images. The company's software can detect a range of medical conditions, including breast cancer, tuberculosis, and pneumonia.

Viz.ai: Viz.ai is a San Francisco-based startup that uses AI to help healthcare providers diagnose and treat stroke. The company's software can analyze medical images and provide healthcare providers with insights that can help them make more accurate diagnoses and provide more effective treatment.

These are just a few examples of the many AI-based healthcare startups that are transforming the healthcare industry. As these startups continue to grow and develop new solutions, they have the potential to revolutionize the way healthcare is delivered, making it more efficient, more effective, and more accessible to patients around the world.

Best Practices In Artificial Intelligence Adoption In Healthcare

As the use of artificial intelligence (AI) in healthcare continues to grow, it is becoming increasingly important for healthcare organizations to adopt best practices to ensure successful implementation and use. In this section we will discuss some of the best practices for AI adoption in healthcare.

Set clear goals and objectives: Before implementing AI, it is important to set clear goals and objectives for its use. This can help ensure that the AI system is aligned with the organization's overall mission and strategy. Goals and objectives should be specific, measurable, achievable, relevant, and time-bound (SMART) to ensure that they are realistic and achievable.

Develop a strong data strategy: Data is a critical component of

AI systems, and it is important to develop a strong data strategy to ensure that the right data is collected, analyzed, and used to train the AI algorithms. The data strategy should include clear policies and procedures for data collection, storage, and use, as well as protocols for data sharing and privacy.

Involve stakeholders early on: To ensure successful AI adoption, it is important to involve all stakeholders early in the process. This can include clinicians, IT professionals, data scientists, patients, and other relevant stakeholders. By involving stakeholders in the design and implementation process, you can ensure that the AI system is user-friendly, effective, and meets the needs of all stakeholders.

Build a strong IT infrastructure: AI systems require a robust IT infrastructure to support their development, implementation, and use. This includes hardware, software, and networking infrastructure that can handle the large volumes of data that AI systems require.

Develop a governance framework: To ensure ethical and responsible use of AI systems, it is important to develop a governance framework that outlines the roles and responsibilities of all stakeholders, as well as policies and procedures for ethical and responsible AI use.

Implement strong security measures: AI systems can pose security risks if not properly secured. It is important to implement strong security measures to protect against data breaches and other security threats. This includes encryption, firewalls, access controls, and other security measures.

Ensure regulatory compliance: AI systems in healthcare are subject to various regulations and standards, including HIPAA, GDPR, and others. It is important to ensure regulatory compliance to avoid legal and financial penalties, as well as reputational damage.

Monitor and evaluate the AI system: To ensure that the AI system is effective and meeting its goals and objectives, it is important to monitor and evaluate its performance. This can include measuring the accuracy of AI algorithms, tracking the system's impact on clinical outcomes, and monitoring user satisfaction.

Continuously improve the AI system: AI systems are not static, and it is important to continuously improve and update them to ensure that they remain effective and meet the changing needs of the organization and its stakeholders.

Foster a culture of innovation and continuous learning: AI adoption requires a culture of innovation and continuous learning. This includes encouraging experimentation and risk-taking, as well as providing ongoing training and professional development for staff.

In conclusion, AI adoption in healthcare can provide significant benefits, but it requires careful planning and implementation to ensure success. By following these best practices, healthcare organizations can ensure that their AI systems are effective, ethical, and aligned with their overall mission and strategy.

CHAPTER 10: THE LONG ROAD AHEAD FOR AI IN HEALTHCARE

T he final chapter discusses the long road ahead for AI in healthcare. It explores the barriers to AI adoption in healthcare, including cultural, technical, and financial barriers. The chapter also discusses the societal and ethical implications of AI in healthcare, including the need to address bias and disparities in AI healthcare. Additionally, the chapter highlights the importance of interdisciplinary collaboration in AI healthcare and the need for robust data governance and infrastructure.

Barriers to AI Adoption in Healthcare

Despite the potential benefits of AI in healthcare, the adoption of these technologies has been slow and faced several barriers. In this section we will explore some of the most significant barriers to AI adoption in healthcare.

Data Quality and Availability: One of the biggest barriers to AI adoption in healthcare is the quality and availability of data. Healthcare data is often fragmented, incomplete, and stored in multiple disparate systems. This can make it challenging for AI systems to access and analyze the data they need to provide accurate predictions and recommendations. To address this barrier, healthcare organizations need to invest in data integration, quality assurance, and standardization initiatives.

Lack of Interoperability: Interoperability refers to the ability of different healthcare systems to communicate and exchange information seamlessly. The lack of interoperability can hinder the adoption of AI in healthcare by limiting the ability of AI systems to access and analyze data from different sources. To overcome this barrier, healthcare organizations need to prioritize interoperability initiatives, such as adopting standard data exchange protocols and interfaces.

Cost: AI technologies can be expensive to implement and maintain, which can be a significant barrier to adoption, particularly for smaller healthcare organizations. The cost of AI adoption can include hardware and software infrastructure, data storage, maintenance, and personnel training. To address this barrier, healthcare organizations can explore options for shared infrastructure and collaborative partnerships to reduce the costs of adoption.

Regulatory and Legal Concerns: Healthcare is a heavily regulated industry, and the adoption of AI technologies can raise concerns around privacy, security, and liability. Regulatory frameworks and guidelines may not be designed to address the unique challenges and risks of AI in healthcare, which can create uncertainty and hesitation among healthcare providers. To address this barrier, healthcare organizations need to work closely with regulatory bodies to ensure that AI technologies comply with applicable regulations and standards.

Cultural Resistance: Another barrier to AI adoption in healthcare is cultural resistance. Healthcare providers and staff may be hesitant to adopt new technologies, particularly if they perceive that they will disrupt established workflows or threaten their jobs. To address this barrier, healthcare organizations need to prioritize change management initiatives that involve staff at all levels of the organization, including training and education programs, communication strategies, and incentives.

Lack of Trust: AI technologies can make mistakes, which can erode trust in these systems among healthcare providers and patients. Lack of trust can hinder adoption by limiting the willingness of healthcare providers to rely on AI systems for clinical decision-making. To address this barrier, healthcare organizations need to prioritize transparency and explainability in AI systems. This can include providing clear explanations of how AI systems work, what data they use, and how they arrive at their predictions or recommendations.

Integration with Existing Workflows: Integrating AI systems with existing clinical workflows can be challenging, particularly if these workflows are already complex and heavily manual. To address this barrier, healthcare organizations need to prioritize workflow analysis and optimization initiatives, such as identifying opportunities for automation and redesigning workflows to incorporate AI systems.

Societal and Ethical Implications of AI in Healthcare

Artificial intelligence (AI) has the potential to transform healthcare by improving patient outcomes, reducing costs, and increasing efficiency. However, the widespread adoption of AI in healthcare raises several ethical and societal concerns that need to be addressed. In this section we will discuss some of the key ethical and societal implications of AI in healthcare.

Bias and Discrimination: One of the biggest concerns regarding the use of AI in healthcare is the potential for bias and discrimination. AI algorithms can be biased if the data used to train them is biased. For example, if a dataset used to train an AI algorithm only includes data from a specific population, it may not be accurate when applied to other populations. This can lead to discrimination in healthcare, where certain groups may be disadvantaged by the use of AI algorithms.

Privacy and Security: Another major concern with the use of AI in healthcare is privacy and security. The use of AI algorithms requires large amounts of sensitive data, including patient data. This data needs to be protected from unauthorized access, theft, or misuse. Healthcare organizations need to ensure that proper security measures are in place to protect patient data.

Autonomy and Responsibility: AI in healthcare raises questions about autonomy and responsibility. Who is responsible when an AI algorithm makes a mistake? How much control should we give AI over healthcare decisions? These questions are particularly important in situations where an AI algorithm makes a life or death decision.

Transparency and Explainability: AI algorithms can be complex, making it difficult to understand how they work and why they make certain decisions. Healthcare organizations need to ensure that AI algorithms are transparent and explainable. This is particularly important in situations where an AI algorithm makes a decision that affects a patient's health.

Informed Consent: The use of AI in healthcare raises questions about informed consent. Patients may not fully understand how AI is being used in their care or what data is being collected. Healthcare organizations need to ensure that patients are fully informed about how their data is being used and have the opportunity to opt-out of data collection if they choose.

Social Impact: The adoption of AI in healthcare has the potential to widen the gap between those who can afford healthcare and those who cannot. The cost of developing and implementing AI algorithms may be prohibitively expensive for some healthcare organizations, which could result in unequal access to healthcare.

Professional Autonomy: The use of AI in healthcare also raises questions about professional autonomy. Healthcare professionals may feel that their professional judgment is being replaced by AI algorithms. It is important to ensure that healthcare professionals are fully involved in the development and implementation of AI algorithms to ensure that they are effective and do not undermine professional autonomy.

Liability and Insurance: The use of AI in healthcare raises questions about liability and insurance. Who is responsible if an AI algorithm makes a mistake? Who pays for any damages that result from an AI algorithm? These questions need to be addressed before AI is widely adopted in healthcare.

Job Loss: The use of AI in healthcare may also lead to job loss for healthcare professionals. Some tasks that are currently performed by healthcare professionals may be automated by AI algorithms. It is important to ensure that healthcare professionals are retrained for new roles or provided with other opportunities to avoid job loss.

Addressing Bias And Disparities In Artificial Intelligence Healthcare

Artificial intelligence (AI) has the potential to revolutionize healthcare by enabling faster and more accurate diagnoses, personalized treatment plans, and improved patient outcomes.

However, the algorithms and data used to develop AI applications are not immune to bias and can perpetuate existing disparities in healthcare. The use of biased AI algorithms can result in incorrect diagnoses, ineffective treatment plans, and perpetuate health disparities.

Addressing bias and disparities in AI healthcare is critical to ensure that these technologies do not further exacerbate healthcare disparities. This section will explore the causes of bias in AI healthcare, the potential consequences of biased AI algorithms, and strategies for addressing bias and disparities in AI healthcare.

Causes of Bias in AI Healthcare

Bias can occur at several stages in the development and deployment of AI healthcare applications. One of the primary causes of bias is biased training data. AI algorithms are only as unbiased as the data used to train them. If the training data is biased, the AI algorithm will learn that bias and perpetuate it in its decision-making. Biases in training data can arise from several sources, including historical data that reflects past discrimination, systematic underreporting of certain groups, and the underrepresentation of certain groups in the data.

Another cause of bias in AI healthcare is the design of the algorithm. The design of the algorithm can introduce bias if it is based on assumptions or prior knowledge that reflect existing biases in healthcare. For example, an algorithm that assumes that certain symptoms are more prevalent in one racial group than another may perpetuate existing health disparities.

Consequences of Bias in AI Healthcare

The consequences of biased AI algorithms in healthcare can be severe. Biased algorithms can lead to incorrect diagnoses, inappropriate treatment plans, and perpetuation of health disparities. For example, a study found that an AI algorithm used for skin cancer diagnosis was less accurate in diagnosing cancer in patients with darker skin tones. This is because the algorithm was trained on a dataset that was predominantly composed of images of patients with lighter skin tones, leading to biases in the algorithm's decision-making.

Bias in AI healthcare can also perpetuate existing health disparities. For example, if an algorithm is biased against certain racial or socioeconomic groups, these groups may be less likely to receive the care they need or may receive suboptimal treatment.

Strategies for Addressing Bias and Disparities in AI Healthcare

Addressing bias and disparities in AI healthcare is critical to ensuring that these technologies do not perpetuate healthcare disparities. Here are some strategies for addressing bias and disparities in AI healthcare:

Diversify the training data: One of the most effective ways to address bias in AI healthcare is to diversify the training data. This means including data from a wide range of sources and ensuring that the data is representative of all groups.

Audit AI algorithms for bias: Regularly auditing AI algorithms for bias can help identify and correct biases in the algorithms.

Use explainable AI: Explainable AI algorithms allow users to understand how the algorithm arrived at its decision-making. This can help identify and correct biases in the algorithm.

Engage diverse stakeholders: Engaging diverse stakeholders, including patients, clinicians, and community members, in the design and implementation of AI healthcare applications can help ensure that the algorithms are fair and equitable.

Develop ethical guidelines: Developing ethical guidelines for the use of AI in healthcare can help ensure that the algorithms are used in an ethical and responsible manner.

Furthermore, it is essential to diversify the data used to train AI models to reduce bias. Healthcare organizations should aim to collect data from diverse populations, including minority groups and underserved communities. This will ensure that the AI models are trained on a representative dataset and can provide unbiased and equitable care to all patients.

Another way to address bias and disparities in AI healthcare is to involve diverse stakeholders in the development and deployment of AI technologies. This includes healthcare providers, patients, community advocates, and policymakers. These stakeholders can provide valuable insights into the specific healthcare needs and challenges faced by different communities, and help ensure that AI technologies are developed and implemented in an ethical and equitable manner.

Finally, healthcare organizations should regularly monitor and evaluate their AI systems to identify and address any biases or disparities that may arise. This can involve conducting regular audits, analyzing performance metrics, and soliciting feedback from patients and providers. By taking a proactive approach to bias and disparity detection and correction, healthcare organizations can ensure that their AI technologies are providing high-quality, equitable care to all patients.

In conclusion, AI has the potential to revolutionize healthcare by improving patient outcomes, increasing efficiency, and reducing costs. However, as with any new technology, there are significant societal and ethical implications that must be considered. Addressing bias and disparities in AI healthcare is critical to ensuring that these technologies are developed and implemented in an ethical and equitable manner.

The Need for Interdisciplinary Collaboration in AI Healthcare

As the use of artificial intelligence (AI) in healthcare continues to grow, it is becoming increasingly clear that effective implementation and adoption require interdisciplinary collaboration. The development of AI systems that can truly benefit patients and healthcare providers requires expertise from a variety of fields, including computer science, data analytics, healthcare management, and clinical medicine.

Interdisciplinary collaboration is essential to ensure that AI healthcare solutions are tailored to the specific needs of patients and healthcare providers, and that they are designed and implemented in a way that is both safe and effective. This chapter will explore the importance of interdisciplinary collaboration in AI healthcare, and how it can be fostered and sustained.

The Benefits of Interdisciplinary Collaboration

Interdisciplinary collaboration can help ensure that AI healthcare solutions are developed and implemented in a way that meets the needs of patients and healthcare providers. By bringing together experts from a range of disciplines, interdisciplinary teams can better understand the complexities of healthcare and develop more effective solutions.

For example, computer scientists can work with clinicians to develop AI algorithms that are more effective at diagnosing disease or predicting outcomes. Data scientists can help ensure that the data used to train AI models is accurate and representative of the patient population. Healthcare managers can ensure that AI systems are integrated into existing healthcare workflows in a way that is seamless and minimizes disruption.

Interdisciplinary collaboration can also help ensure that AI healthcare solutions are developed and implemented in an ethical and socially responsible manner. By bringing together experts from a range of fields, interdisciplinary teams can better identify and address potential ethical and societal concerns.

Challenges to Interdisciplinary Collaboration

While interdisciplinary collaboration is essential to the development of effective AI healthcare solutions, there are several challenges to achieving effective collaboration.

One of the main challenges is the siloing of expertise in different disciplines. Experts in computer science, data analytics, and healthcare management may not be familiar with the unique challenges and complexities of clinical medicine, and vice versa. This can lead to a lack of understanding and communication between different disciplines, making it difficult to develop effective solutions.

Another challenge is the time and resource constraints faced by healthcare providers and researchers. Developing effective AI healthcare solutions requires a significant investment of time and resources, and interdisciplinary collaboration can be difficult to sustain in the face of competing priorities.

Fostering and Sustaining Interdisciplinary Collaboration

Despite these challenges, there are several strategies that can be used to foster and sustain interdisciplinary collaboration in AI healthcare.

One strategy is to create interdisciplinary teams that include experts from a range of fields. By bringing together experts with different backgrounds and areas of expertise, teams can ensure that all perspectives are considered and that solutions are developed in a comprehensive and integrated manner.

Another strategy is to provide training and education to help experts in different fields better understand each other's perspectives and challenges. This can help build trust and improve communication between different disciplines, making it easier to collaborate effectively.

Collaborative spaces can also be created to facilitate interdisciplinary collaboration. These spaces can include virtual platforms, such as online forums and collaborative workspaces, as well as physical spaces where interdisciplinary teams can meet and work together.

Finally, funding and resource allocation can be used to incentivize interdisciplinary collaboration. For example, funding agencies can prioritize proposals that involve interdisciplinary collaboration, and healthcare organizations can allocate resources to support interdisciplinary teams working on AI healthcare solutions.

In addition to collaboration between healthcare professionals, AI experts, and policymakers, interdisciplinary collaboration between the fields of computer science, engineering, statistics, and ethics is also essential. Each of these fields brings a unique perspective and set of skills to the development and implementation of AI in healthcare.

Computer scientists and engineers are responsible for designing and building the AI systems themselves, ensuring their technical feasibility and scalability. They also play a key role in developing algorithms for tasks such as data processing and analysis, natural language processing, and machine learning. Statisticians are critical for ensuring that AI systems are reliable, accurate, and robust. They help to develop and evaluate statistical models that underpin many AI applications, and they can help to identify and mitigate sources of bias or error in the data.

Ethicists are important in ensuring that AI in healthcare is developed and implemented in an ethical and responsible manner. They can help to identify potential ethical issues and provide guidance on how to address them. Ethical considerations in AI healthcare include issues such as privacy, informed consent, fairness, transparency, and accountability.

Interdisciplinary collaboration can help to ensure that AI in healthcare is developed and implemented in a way that maximizes its benefits while minimizing its risks. It can help to ensure that the technology is technically sound, reliable, and accurate, while also being ethical, transparent, and accountable. It can also help to ensure that the technology is accessible and affordable, so that it can benefit all patients, regardless of their socioeconomic status or geographic location.

Collaboration between these disciplines can take many forms, including joint research projects, interdisciplinary training programs, and interdisciplinary conferences and workshops. It can also involve the development of interdisciplinary teams that work together on specific AI healthcare projects, bringing together experts from each of these fields to ensure that all perspectives are represented.

Overall, interdisciplinary collaboration is critical for the development and implementation of AI in healthcare. It can help to ensure that the technology is developed and implemented in an ethical and responsible manner, while also maximizing its benefits for patients and healthcare providers. By bringing together experts from different fields, we can work together to ensure that AI in healthcare is safe, effective, and accessible to all who need it.

The Importance Of Robust Data Governance And Infrastructure

The success of AI in healthcare relies heavily on the availability of high-quality, diverse, and well-curated data. Without access to robust data, AI algorithms cannot learn effectively, and their predictions may be inaccurate or biased. Therefore, the importance of robust data governance and infrastructure cannot be overstated.

Data governance refers to the overall management of data, including its availability, usability, and security. In healthcare, this includes the policies and procedures governing the collection, storage, use, and sharing of patient data. Robust data governance ensures that data is collected ethically, stored securely, and used appropriately. It also helps to ensure that data is accurate, complete, and reliable.

To support AI in healthcare, it is essential to have a robust infrastructure that can store, process, and analyze large amounts of data. This includes hardware, software, and networking components that are designed to work together seamlessly. The infrastructure must also be scalable and adaptable to accommodate future growth and changes in technology.

One of the key challenges of data governance and infrastructure in healthcare is the need to balance patient privacy with the benefits of data sharing. Patients have a right to privacy and control over their health data. However, to develop accurate and effective AI algorithms, researchers and developers need access to diverse and comprehensive datasets. This creates a tension between privacy and data sharing that must be managed carefully.

To address this challenge, organizations should develop policies and procedures that govern the collection, use, and sharing of patient data. These policies should be transparent and communicated clearly to patients, healthcare providers, and researchers. They should also ensure that patient data is de-identified to protect privacy while maintaining the usefulness of the data for research and AI development.

Another challenge of data governance and infrastructure in healthcare is the need for interoperability. Healthcare data is often siloed within different systems and organizations, making it difficult to share and analyze. To support AI in healthcare, data must be standardized and accessible across different systems and organizations. This requires collaboration and coordination among healthcare providers, researchers, and policymakers.

In conclusion, robust data governance and infrastructure are essential to the success of AI in healthcare. Healthcare organizations must balance patient privacy with the benefits of data sharing to support AI development and research. By following best practices and investing in data security and cybersecurity measures, organizations can ensure that patient data is used ethically, securely, and effectively to improve patient outcomes and advance healthcare research.

The future of AI in healthcare is exciting and full of potential. As technology continues to advance, we can expect to see AI play an increasingly important role in the diagnosis, treatment, and management of a wide range of health conditions. However, it is important to approach the adoption of AI in healthcare with caution and a commitment to ethical and responsible use. By working together to develop robust standards and guidelines, we can ensure that the benefits of AI in healthcare are realized while minimizing potential risks and challenges.

ACKNOWLEDGEMENT

This book is the result of the hard work and dedication of many individuals who have supported and encouraged me throughout the journey. Their contributions have been invaluable and have helped shape this book into what it is today.

First and foremost, I would like to express my deep gratitude to the healthcare professionals and researchers who have dedicated their lives to improving the health and well-being of others. Their passion and commitment to advancing the field of healthcare have been a constant source of inspiration for me.

I would also like to extend my heartfelt thanks to the experts in the field of artificial intelligence who generously shared their knowledge and insights with me. Their expertise and guidance have been instrumental in helping me to navigate the complex landscape of AI in healthcare.

I am grateful to the Amazon team and Kindle platform that provided me with the opportunity to share my thoughts and research with a wider audience. Their technologies have been invaluable in bringing this book to fruition.

Finally, I would like to thank my family and friends for their unwavering support and encouragement throughout this journey. Their love and encouragement have sustained me through the long hours of research and writing, and I could not have done it without them.

To all of you, I offer my deepest appreciation and thanks. Your contributions have made this book possible, and I hope it will serve as a valuable resource for all those interested in the transformative impact of artificial intelligence on healthcare.

Made in the USA
Coppell, TX
01 November 2023